List of Contents

Preface

Most great hymns have a story. Knowing the story behind a hymn helps us appreciate more deeply its beauty and power. In most cases the creation of a hymn was intensely personal, a reaction to some life experience. They wrote from the depths of their heart having no idea that one day the Christian Church would sing their songs.

Francis Schaeffer said, 'A wonderful companion to the Bible is a good hymn book.' Indeed, hymnology contains a wealth of valuable and challenging information to enrich our spiritual lives. For this reason this book is published, hoping it might open the door to a deeper appreciation of the wonder of a hymn.

The Publishers

Abide With Me

Henry Francis Lyte

I n the Christian church there's a hymn for every occasion and that's a good thing.

There are hymns of praise and thanksgiving; uplifting the heart. There are hymns of testimony and witness; proclaiming the truth. There are hymns which anticipate heaven and encourage the saints to press on to glory. And there are hymns for special occasions like Christmas, Easter, weddings and even funerals.

All of us who have suffered the grief which comes when death enters the home will understand the sense of utter helplessness which grips the bereaved.

It's inevitable that the angel of death will visit every family eventually, so when he does it's important to provide the sorrowing ones with all the support and encouragement that's possible.

Here's a hymn which does just that.

Abide with me, must have been sung at more funerals than any other.

There's something particularly solemn about a funeral church filled with men sounding out the strains of this moving hymn. It seems to promote a special reverence at such times; to call down the very hush of heaven.

The man who wrote the words seemed to sense the overlapping of time and eternity; of life and death.

Henry Francis Lyte was the pastor of a little seaside congregation for more than twenty-four years. The members of the church, at Lower Brixham, Devonshire, on England's south coast, were husky, hardy, seafaring men; well used to the ravages of wind and weather.

Well used, also, to the stark trauma of tragedy at sea and the bitter cup of sudden death. The fisherfolk living in such areas of these islands are sadly familiar with the strains of *Abide with me*.

Pastor Lyte, however, didn't enjoy anything resembling good health. Indeed he was fail and sickly. At length it was suggested that a change of climate would be of benefit, and accordingly, he prepared to move to the sunny shores of southern Europe. The doctor gave him the grim news that he had the dreaded 'consumption,' and advised him, 'soak up all the sun you can; it's your only hope of recovery'.

With more than a heavy heart the Reverend Lyte prepared for his journey.

Now ministers become attached to their pulpits; and well nigh addicted to the ministry of the Word of God. Henry Francis Lyte was no exception and so, on the Sunday before he was due to depart, in September 1847, he ascended the pulpit steps once more.

His people wondered if he would have the strength to stand behind the sacred desk: or if he would have the voice to speak!

However, with determination he rallied his remaining energies and addressed his beloved people thus:

'I stand among you today as alive from the dead, that I may hope to impress upon you to prepare for that solemn hour which must come to us all, by a time acquaintance with the death of Christ.'

And so he begged them once more to put their trust in the Saviour.

Later he served at the Lord's table in a farewell communion feast with his now tearful congregation; and then lovingly committed them to the Lord in prayer.

At home, that same evening, anguish poured from his grief-stricken soul and in search of solace he penned the words of his now famous hymn:

> *Abide with me; fast falls the eventide;*
> *The darkness deepens; Lord, with me abide*
> *When other helpers fail and comforts flee,*
> *Help of the helpless, O abide with me.*

Next day the weary servant of God set sail for Nice in the hope of better health. Sadly, however, it was not to be, for just two short months later, on November 20th, he passed into the presence of his Lord with the words, 'joy' and 'peace' upon his lips.

The early ministry of Henry Francis Lyte had ended. He had gone to his everlasting rest and to his eternal reward. But, thankfully, he left behind as good a legacy as any man could ever hope to leave - a ministry faithfully completed and a great hymn, still sung by millions.

All Creatures Of Our God And King

Francis of Assisi

One of my favourite hymn tunes is associated with what has been called, 'Nature's Hymn of Praise,' namely, *'All Creatures Of Our God And King.'* It was written by Francis of Assisi. The melody is of unknown origin, but was first published in a hymnal in 1623.

Francis was born into the carefree life of a wealthy Italian family in 1182. At an early age he was converted to Jesus Christ. Renouncing his life of ease, he became an itinerant evangelist who roamed through the countryside, working with the peasants and preaching to them. He gathered about him a large group of followers with whom he toured the Mediterranean lands for fourteen years. The message he proclaimed was that love for Christ leads to a life of sacrifice and of brotherly love among men.

This 'patron saint of animals' came to love God's world of nature, probably because he lived a simple life so close to it. His hymn expresses the truth that all creation praises its Creator. It may have been based on Psalm 145:10,11: 'All thy works shall praise thee, O Lord ... They shall speak of the glory of thy kingdom, and talk of thy power.'

It is said that Francis wrote these words during the summer of 1225 when he was very ill and losing his sight.

All creatures of our God and King,
Lift up your voice and with us sing,
Alleluia! Alleluia!
Thou burning sun with golden beam,
Thou silver moon with softer gleam!
O praise Him, O praise Him,
Alleluia! Alleluia! Alleluia!

All People That on Earth Do Dwell

William Kethe

What a magnificent start William Kethe's version of Psalm 100 makes to a hymn book. His four stately verses set to the *Old Hundreth* have graced many notable occasions, and form one of the most successful of the adaptations of the Psalms.

Although he was a Scot, William Kethe may have written his hymn in the green and pleasant vale of Blackmoor in Dorset, deep in the heart of rural England, for in the years between 1560 and 1570 he was nominally Rector of Childe Okeford near Blandford. There is no memorial of him in the old church with its eye on the Dorset downs, but his hymn is worth a good many brass tablets.

Before he had this Dorset living he was mixed up in the 'Reformation troubles' on the Continent and was a kind of messenger between England and the exiles in Basle and Strasbourg. Many of his Psalm versions were published in Geneva (perhaps this one was), and reached Scotland, too. But *All People* is the most renowned of his versions and it is easy to see why.

If you read Psalm 100 alongside the hymn, you will see that Kethe takes the salient point of the Psalm, and, without fuss or decoration, puts them into verse. The Psalm in the Authorised Version takes five verses; Kethe does it in four - four of the greatest verses of praise in the English language.

All people that on earth do dwell,
Sing to the Lord with cheerful voice;
Him serve with mirth, his praise forth tell,
Come ye before him and rejoice.

Amazing Grace

John Newton

March the 21st is a day to be remembered by me. I have never suffered it to pass wholly unnoticed since the year 1748. On that day the Lord sent from on high and delivered me from deep waters.'

So wrote John Newton in his autobiography, aptly titled, *Out of the Depths*. It was on that memorable day that newton came into a personal, saving relationship with Jesus Christ.

Ever since he had been a young boy, John Newton had dreamed of following in the footsteps of his father, a sea captain. At the tender age of eleven he joined his father's ship which sailed the warm, blue waters of the Mediterranean and for the best part of the next twenty years that ambition was realised.

Life for the young mariner was by no means a matter of 'plain sailing', however. Growing up, he soon learned the ways of wickedness - to his terrible cost. He fought with his father, clashed with his employers, was flogged for desertion, and finally ended up in jail.

Punishment did nothing to change him, and on his release he continued his immoral living with unrestrained debauchery.

Eventually, by a long sequence of tragic events, he found himself employed in one of the most despicable of all trades in those days, slavery.

What a poor, miserable, wretched sinner John Newton turned out to be! And yet, it was in the Lord's great plan to deliver him and make something of him.

Here's how it happened. And if you know anything about ships and the sea you'll be able to put yourself in Newton's shoes; or should it be sea-boots!

The year was 1748 and it was the month of March, when the seas are at their most violent.

A raging storm was blowing of the North-West coast of Ireland and Newton and his ship were caught in the midst of it.

Thundering waves pounded the helpless vessel again and again, crashing over the decks, filling it with water and threatening to send it and its crew to the bottom. Newton and his ship-mates strained at the pumps but it seemed a hopeless task as the mighty waves broke relentlessly over them.

The ship was just about to break up when Newton, fearing for his very life, saw a ray of hope.

'If this will not do, then the Lord have mercy on us,' he cried, and then the thought of 'mercy' came to him again.

'What mercy can there be for me,' he wondered, but, nevertheless, began to pray in earnest. In a remarkable way God answered and the storm was abated.

That 'memorable day' as Newton later referred to it was March 21st 1748 and he was then 23 years old.

He finally gave up seafaring in 1755 and was appointed tide surveyor at Liverpool where he became acquainted with George Whitefiled and John Wesley.

He began the study of Greek and Hebrew and in 1758 applied to the archbishop of York for ordination to the Church of England ministry but was refused.

However, in 1764, he was offered the curacy of the parish of St. Peter and St. Paul at Olney in Buckinghamshire, and was ordained by the bishop of Lincoln.

Three years later the poet William Cowper, of whom we'll hear later in this book, settled in the parish and the two men became firm friends.

Together they published Olney Hymns, for which Newton himself wrote a number of pieces, including How Sweet The Name Of Jesus Sounds, and, most famous of all, Amazing Grace.

Amazing Grace has been a firm favourite with Christians everywhere for many years. I'm sure it will always remain so. It is, after all, Newton's own testimony in song, telling the marvellous story of his transformation from spiritual blindness to sight - and all through grace.

In 1779 Newton left Olney to become rector of St. Mary Woolnoth, in London. There he continued to exercise an important and fruitful ministry for the remaining 28 years of his life.

Living in the capital city and close to the seat of power in government he was able to influence many in authority, among them, William Wilberforce, the future leader in the campaign to abolish slavery. That must surely have given the former slave ship captain particular satisfaction.

John Newton was also a great writer of devotional letters. These are widely published and some would say were his greatest contributions to the evangelical movement of those times.

He died in London on December 21st 1807, having served the Lord and his church faithfully for almost 60 years.

Towards the end of his life he often told his audiences, 'My memory is nearly gone but I can remember two things; that I am a great sinner and that Christ is a great Saviour.'

On his tombstone in the churchyard of his former parish at Olney are these words:

John Newton, clerk, once an infidel and libertine, a servant of slaves in Africa, was by the rich mercy of our Lord and Saviour, Jesus Christ, preserved, restored, pardoned and appointed to preach the faith he had long laboured to destroy.

What else can be said other than that John Newton was well qualified to preach and describe God's 'Amazing grace'.

Amazing grace! how sweet the sound,
That saved a wretch like me!
I once was lost, but now am found;
Was blind, but now I see.

'Twas grace that taught my heart to fear,
And grace my fears relieved;
How precious did that grace appear,
The hour I first believed!

Through many dangers, toils and snares
I have already come;
'Tis grace has brought me safe thus far,
And grace will lead me home.

A Mighty Fortress

'Ein Feste Burt Ist ...'

Martin Luther

T he most accurate direct translation of these words is:
'*A sure stronghold our God is he,*
a trusty shield and weapon.
Our help he'll be and set us free
from every ill can happen
that old malicious foe, means us deadly woe
armed with might from Hell
and deepest craft as well
on earth is not his fellow.'
I'm sure you recognise this as the original of *A Mighty Fortress is Our God.*

Martin Luther who wrote the words once said, 'The Devil hates music because he cannot stand gaiety,' and 'Satan can smirk but he cannot laugh; he can sneer but he cannot sing.'

Because he believed in the power of song the great reformer spent a lot of time compiling a hymn book for use in congregational singing.

One writer has said that 'Luther translated the Bible into German so God could speak directly to the people; and provided the hymn so that the people could answer God in their songs.'

Luther is credited with thirty-seven hymns, by far the most popular being, *A Mighty Fortress.*

It was written in 1529 at time when Luther and his followers were going through a particularly rough patch of opposition; with the Emperor, Charles V, seemingly determined to suppress the new movement.

During those days of struggle Luther turned often to Psalm forty six and was greatly encouraged by the words of verse one, '*God is our refuge and strength, a very present help in trouble.*'

Soon a song was inspired, and Luther began in fine style with the bold declaration - 'Ein feste burg ist unswer Gott' - 'A sure stronghold our God is He.' It was Frederick Hedge, in his translation of 1852 who changed this to the more familiar *A Mighty Fortress Is Our God.*

Luther's original composition became immediately popular with the common people of reformation Germany, being sung continually in the streets and chanted by the martyrs as they awaited their grim fate. What a moving sound that must have made!

At this point mention must be made of the music, that rich, melodious - yea, majestic tune which lifts the words and carries them along with all the pomp and grace of a national anthem.

Considerable dispute surrounds the origin of the music, with some attributing it to Luther himself. Others give the honour to the great J.S. Bach; and it's true that Bach did use the tune as the basis of one of his many chorales.

However, Bach was not born until 1685, over a hundred and fifty years after Luther's great hymn first appeared. It seems clear then, that Martin Luther rightly deserves the credit, if not for the original composition, at least for adapting it, possibly from an old German folk tune.

Much more important than the music however, is the message - and what a message this great hymn has for the people of God!

It turns their eyes and thoughts away from the afflictions of this world, and the opposition of Satanic hosts, and fixes them upon the person of the Lord Jesus - the Lord Sabaoth as Luther so rightly refers to Him in one of the verses ...

Did we in our own strength confide,
Our striving would be losing;
Were not the right Man on our side,
The man of God's own choosing.
Dost ask who that may be?
Christ Jesus, it is He!
Lord Sabaoth is His Name,
From age to age the same;
And he must win the battle.

At Even When The Sun Was Set

Henry Twells

No hymn in the English Language breathes a more genuine piety and sense of prayer than this one. It is surprising that Canon Twells is not remembered by any other hymn that he wrote. But for this one we can be grateful. In the prime of his years (he was born in 1823) from 1856 to 1870 he was headmaster of a great London school, the Godolphin at Hammersmith, and was later an honorary canon of Peterborough Cathedral.

The first line of his hymn as printed above is now generally accepted instead of *At Even Ere The Sun Was Set* although this line falls more gently on the ear. But *when* is certainly more Scripturally accurate than *ere* as both Mark 1:32 and Luke 4:40 prefer *when*. And Jewish custom supports it. No group of sick and diseased people would have fathered in the way that Canon Twells describes until the sun had set on the Sabbath day.

It is a pity that one of Canon Twell's verse is so often missed out in modern hymn collections:

> And some are pressed with worldly care,
> And some are tired with sinful doubt;
> And some such grievous passions tear,
> That only Thou canst cast them out.

A verse most apposite to modern life, and a prayer that most of us can make our own.

Battle Hymn of the Republic

Julia Ward Howe

At the age of ninety-two, Julia Ward Howe received an honorary degree from Smith College. As she was wheeled onto the platform, she received a standing ovation. After the presentation, the organist struck a chord, and the standing audience began to sing, *Mine Eyes Have Seen The Glory Of The Coming Of The Lord.*

In 1861, after the Civil War had begun, Dr. Samuel G. Howe, his wife, Julia Ward Howe, their pastor from Boston, and the governor of Massachusetts were witnessing a review of northern troops under General McClellan near Washington D.C. There was a sudden movement of the enemy, and the Howe party hurried back to Washington passing troop after troop all singing *John Brown's body lies amouldering in the grave.* They heard it over and over.

When they were out of danger, Dr. Clarke, the minister, turned to Mrs. Howe. 'That's a stirring melody, Julia, but can't you write better words for it?'

Mrs. Howe went to bed that night and slept quite soundly. Suddenly she awoke early in the morning and found her mind twirling with words. She told herself to get up and write down the verses lest she fall asleep again and forget them.

In the dimness of the dawn, she found a pen and began to put down on a scrap of paper the verses to the immortal *Battle Hymn of the Republic.*

When she returned to Boston, she decided to show her poem to the editor of *The Atlantic Monthly.* He accepted it, suggested the title, and paid her five dollars.

Soon after it was published, it became one of the greatest songs to come out of the Civil War. It has continued to find its way into practically ever hymnal published since.

Julia Ward Howe was born in 1816 into a prominent New York City family. Her mother was a poet of some ability. A combination of tutors and private schools provided her with an excellent education in literature and languages. By the age of seventeen, she was writing poetry for leading magazines.

In 1843 she married Dr. Samuel G. Howe, the director of the Massachusetts State School for the Blind. The Howes had six children. Both she and her husband were sympathetic toward the Abolitionist Movement and became enthusiastic crusaders.

After the Civil War, Mrs. Howe actively crusaded for the unpopular cause of women suffrage, helping to found the American Woman Suffrage Association. Later she worked for prison reform and visited wounded servicemen in hospitals. These experiences caused her to think deeply about the agony, the suffering, the dreadful price of war.

Shortly after the Battle Hymn of the Republic appeared in the Atlantic Monthly, Chaplain McCabe, an army volunteer from Ohio, read the poem in the magazine. He was able to memorise it by singing it through a few times.

Later he was captured by the Confederates and put in prison in Richmond. News came to the prisoners that the Union troops had lost thousands of men in battle. It is hard enough to be in prison, but believing they were on the losing side, they felt all hope was gone.

Suddenly someone burst into the prison to announce that the report had been an error and that the Union soldiers had been victorious. Chaplain McCabe began to sing, *Mine eyes have seen the glory of the coming of the Lord*. The other prisoners joined in on the chorus, *Glory, glory, hallelujah!*

When Chaplain McCabe was released from prison, he went to Washington to speak to a Christian group. There he told about all the prisoners singing the Battle Hymn of the Republic. The audience requested that he sing it for them. When he finished, President Lincoln, with tears streaming down his faced, asked him to sing it again.

Mine eyes have seen the glory
of the coming of the Lord;
He is trampling out the vintage
where the grapes of wrath are stored!
He hath loosed the fateful lightning
of His terrible swift sword;
His truth is marching on.

Be Still My Soul

Kathrarina von Schlegel

Very little is known of the origins of this hymn or of its author. Katharina von Schlegel, born in 1697 was probably head of a Women's House of the Evangelical Lutheran Church at Cothen in Germany. She was also probably associated with the little ducal court of Cothen. Her hymn was discovered and translated by Jane L. Borthwick (1813-97), and its popularity today is no doubt due to its setting to Sibelius' famous melody Finlandia.

The hymn is an expression of deep piety and trust in God, a fine example of the German pietistic experience.

Be still, my soul: the Lord is on thy side;
Bear patiently the cross of grief or pain;
Leave to thy God to order and provide;
In every change He faithful will remain.
Be still, my soul: thy best, thy heavenly Friend
Through thorny ways leads to a joyful end.

Be still, my soul: thy God doth undertake
To guide the future as He has the past.
Thy hope, thy confidence let nothing shake;
All now mysterious shall be bright at last.
Be still, my soul: the waves and wind still know
His voice who ruled them while He dwelt below.

Be Thou My Vision

Irish traditional

The hymn *Be Thou My Vision* is a prayer that we may accept Christ as our pattern, our hero, our ideal. Our adoration is told in these names and phrases: Lord of my heart, my best thought, my wisdom, my true word, my great Father, mine inheritance, my treasure and finally, heart of my own heart.

The original version of this hymn was written by an unknown Irish Christian in the eighth century. The tune is an Irish folk melody.

Be Thou my Vision, O Lord of my heart;
Nought be all else to me, save that Thou art -
Thou my best thought, by day or by night,
Waking or sleeping, Thy presence my light.

Be Thou my Vision, and Thou my true Word;
I ever with Thee and Thou with me, Lord;
Thou my great Father, and I Thy true son;
Thou in me dwelling and I with Thee one.

Riches I need not, nor man's empty praise,
Thou mine inheritance, now and always:
Thou and Thou only, first in my heart,
High King of heaven, my Treasure Thou art.

High King of heaven, my victory won,
May I reach heaven's joy, O bright heaven's Sun!
Heart of my own heart, whatever befall,
Still be my Vision, O Ruler of all.

Bless This House

Helen Taylor

When does a song become a hymn? It looks as if Helen Taylor's popular *Bless This House* has a foot in both camps. In Britain, where Helen Taylor wrote it in 1927, with musical setting by May Brahe, her song is famous as a solo:

Bless this house, O Lord, we pray
Make it safe by night and day:
Bless these walls so firm and stout
Keeping want and trouble out.

Bless the roof and chimneys tall
Let Thy peace lie over all:
Bless this door, that it may prove
Ever open to joy and love.

In the United States it is frequently near the top in radio choices of popular hymns. During Thanksgiving Week especially - America's great home festival - it is one of the most played works.

John McCormack helped to make the song famous by his fine singing and recording of it. When McCormack appeared for the 25th season at the London Ballad Concerts in 1935 he asked Mr. Leslie Boosey to find him a suitable song to introduce. He was shown the song *Bless The House*, but with a singer's instinct for a word he suggested an alteration to *Bless This House*. So the title and the opening words were changed, and the song became immediately popular - particularly during the heavy bombing of British homes during the war.

Helen Taylor, the song writer, was the wife of Mr. Sydney H. Rothschild and was born in Britain in 1875 and died in 1943. Two other famous songs of hers are *I Passed By Your Window* and *Come To The Fair*. Helen Taylor's simple lines of sincere homely sentiment make their instant appeal:

> *Bless these windows shining bright,*
> *Letting in God's heavenly light;*
> *Bless the hearth ablazing there,*
> *With smoke ascending like a prayer.*
>
> *Bless the people here within,*
> *Keep them pure and free from sin;*
> *Bless us all that we my be ,*
> *Fit, O Lord, to dwell with thee.*

Blessed Assurance

Fanny Crosby

The writer of this great hymn, Fanny Crosby, lived to be almost ninety-five years of age and during that time penned the staggering total of over eight thousand sacred songs and hymns.

What is even more remarkable is the fact that this great life's work was accomplished without the aid of eyesight.

When she was only six weeks old, baby Fanny Crosby caught a cold. Her eyes became terribly inflamed and a country doctor prescribed, of all things, a mustard poultice. The desperate remedy resulted in the child's immediate blindness.

Even the then famous New York Surgeon, Dr. Valentine Mott, could do nothing to help her. Showing Fanny and her widowed mother to the door after his examination which confirmed the hopelessness of her condition he was heard to lament, 'Poor little blind girl!'

However, Fanny Crosby was to turn her affliction into an asset and in later years looked upon her blindness as a blessing.

When she was twelve she entered the New York Institute for the Blind and was so successful as a student that in later years, from 1847 until 1858 she taught in the same school.

She began writing poetry at the age of eight with this simple little verse:

Oh, what a happy child I am,
Although I cannot see!
I am resolved that in this world
Contented I will be.

It was much later, however, while working at the Institute for the Blind, that she began to develop her talent for writing and to turn it into something profitable.

Her popular, secular verse made her name famous. Such songs as *Rosalie The Prairie Flower* and *There's Music In The Air,* were set to music by composer George F. Root and sold in sheet music by the thousands.

An interesting sidelight here is that the male secretary of the Institute's superintendent used to take down the lines of verse as Fanny Crosby dictated them. In fact, on at least one occasion they were both reprimanded for this 'waste of the school's time.'

That school secretary was called Grover Cleveland and many a time in later years he was to set aside the important affairs of the presidency to take dictation from his welcome White House guest, Fanny Crosby.

She was 44 years old when she gave up secular songs to devote her full energies to sacred compositions. From her prolific pen flowed such popular and all time favourites as *Near The Cross, Safe In The Arms Of Jesus, Rescue The Perishing, Pass Me Not O Gentle Saviour* and *Blessed Assurance.*

The story behind the writing of *Blessed assurance* is simple, yet interesting.

One day Miss Crosby was in the home of her friend Mrs Joseph F. Knapp. In the Knapp home was installed what was believed to be the largest pipe organ ever placed in a private dwelling. However, on this particular day Mrs Knapp called her guest over to the piano to listen to a new melody she had just composed. After playing the tune a few times she asked, 'What do you think the tune says?'

'Blessed assurance Jesus is mine', answered Fanny Crosby, and then, drawing from her vast storehouse of Scripture knowledge, continued with

Oh what a foretaste of glory divine
Heir of salvation, purchase of God
Born of His Spirit, washed in His blood.

In a very short time a new sacred song was born with words by Fanny Crosby and music by Mrs J. F. Knapp.

Although written as far back as 1873 *Blessed Assurance* still remains a firm favourite with Christians everywhere.

I have personal, vivid memories of it being sung rousingly at summer beach-meetings and in the open air; its sweet and lively strains wafting over the clear air and telling out the testimony of those who sang ...

This is my story, this is my song,
Praising my Saviour all the day long.

Blest Be The Tie That Binds

John Fawcett

Blest be the tie that binds
Our hearts in Christian love;
The fellowship of kindred minds
Is like to that above.

Before our Father's throne
We pour our ardent prayers;
Our fears, our hopes, our aims are one,
Our comforts and our cares.

We share our mutual woes;
Our mutual burdens bear;
And often for each other flows
The sympathising tear.

When we asunder part,
It gives us inward pain;
But we shall still be joined in heart,
And hope to meet again.

The Reverend John Fawcett was the minister of the Baptist church at Wainsgate, England. In his time he was one of the greatest scholars in the land and an able preacher. He wrote several books, published a volume of hymns and founded a school for the education and training of young preachers.

An essay on 'Anger' written by him so impressed George III that the king offered him any benefit a monarch could confer.

John Fawcett had been left an orphan at the age of 12. He had to work very hard during his youth, regularly putting in 14 hours a day in what was termed in those days a 'sweat shop'. By candle light he learned to read and studied hard to improve his education.

Ordained at 25 he had taken the little church with its 100 members for a modest salary; paid partly in potatoes and wool.

Now, after seven years, he had received a call to the great Carter Lane church in London and was preparing to make the move.

The day came to say farewell to his congregation. The horse and dray stood outside his house and, one by one, the items of furniture were loaded.

Finally, the last item was hoised up and made secure. The Reverend Fawcett began his round of farewells. There were young couples he had joined in marriage; those whom he had comforted through sickness and trial; the children he has held on his knee; and the old whose sorrows he had shared.

They were a humble people; few of them could either read or write, but they loved their minister and their devotion to him finally overcame.

The drayman was instructed to unload - John Fawcett would stay a little longer. He stayed, in fact, for another 54 years until his death in 1817.

He never did take up the offer from King George III. Commenting on the incident he said he 'needed nothing a king could supply,' so long as he could live among the people he loved ... those humble people whose devotion had inspired him to write his famous hymn.

Break Thou The Bread of Life

Mary Lathbury

Before his mid-week service, the great London preacher G. Campbell Morgan always read the words to the hymn, *Break Thou The Bread Of Life*. The third verse is an excellent prayer for understanding God's truth.

> *O send Thy Spirit, Lord,*
> *Now unto me,*
> *That He may touch my eyes,*
> *And make me see:*
> *Show me the truth concealed*
> *Within Thy Word,*
> *And in Thy Book revealed*
> *I see the Lord.*

Mary Lathbury wrote this hymn. Born in a parsonage in Manchester, New York, she showed artistic tendencies even as a child. She particularly enjoyed drawing pictures of children.

When she graduated from school, she shared an art studio with her sister in New York where she also taught art. Her illustrations in magazines and periodicals made her name widely known. She also wrote books of poetry and illustrated them with sketches.

She enjoyed what she was doing, but she yearned to serve the Lord in a more complete way. The opportunity came when Dr. John Vincent, a Methodist clergyman, asked her to assist him in the Chautauqua Movement as his secretary. He founded the school as a summer instruction session for Sunday School teachers. Its location was ideal - a beautiful wooded area in New York state by the blue waters of Lake Chautauqua.

Dr. Vincent appreciated Mary's artistic talent, competence, and helpfulness. Whenever he wished to have a hymn that would fit into a study session of the Bible, he would ask her to write one. Music played a large part in the meetings.

When seeking inspiration, it was her custom to find a quiet spot overlooking the lake. While praying one day for guidance as to what to write, she began thinking of Christ feeding the five thousand by the Sea of Galilee. From her reflection came the widely known hymn, *Break Thou The Bread Of Life*.

Another hymn she wrote by the shore of Lake Chautauqua was *Day Is Dying In The West*. This beautiful evening hymn quickly became a favourite. It is still sung as Christians gather to praise God and to remember that the Lord is with us now and forever.

Mary Lathbury became known as the 'poet of Chautauqua'. Those who knew her best tell of her indescribable charm, her gentle Christian character and the influence for good she had on other people because of her dedication to the Lord.

She founded a club, the Look-Up Legion, which attracted thousands of boys and girls to Christianity. The foundation rules were: 'Look up and not down; look forward and not back; look out and not in; and lend a hand in Jesus name.'

Break thou the bread of life,
Dear Lord, to me,
As thou didst break the loaves
Beside the sea;
Beyond the sacred page
I seek thee, Lord;
My spirit pants for thee,
O Living Word.

Breathe on Me, Breath Of God

Edwin Hatch

This hymn is a genuine transatlantic one, for Edwin Hatch spent eight most memorable years in Canada, first as professor of classics in Trinity College, Toronto, and then as rector of the High School of Quebec.

Those years from 1859-1867 were a young man's years in Canada, and the peace and beauty of lakes and rivers much have had their effect on the sensitive spirit of Edwin Hatch. His later years in Oxford brought him honour and fame as church historian and theologian.

It was after his death in 1889 that his little book of poems *Towards Fields of Light* was published containing this little gem of prayer to the God the Holy Spirit.

> *Breathe on me, Breath of God,*
> *Fill me with life anew,*
> *That I may love what Thou dost love,*
> *And do what Thou wouldst do.*

It has the shape and light of genuine religious poetry. It lifts naturally,

> *Breath on me, breath of God,*
> *Till I am wholly Thine,*
> *until this earthly part of me*
> *Glows with Thy fire divine.*

and soars to eternity,

> *Breath on me, Breath of God,*
> *So shall I never die,*
> *But live with Thee the perfect life*
> *Of Thine eternity.*

Come Ye Thankful People Come

Henry Alford

O ne of the most beautiful seasons of the year especially for the church, is harvest. I love it! To see the house of God tastefully decorated with the fruits of the field and the flowers of the garden is a sight to gladden any heart. The fruits and flowers are evident tokens of the manifold provisions of God; and it's right that we should have special services of thanksgiving.

Harvest time is also a great opportunity to press home the truths of the Scripture to saint and sinner.

Many a weary child of God has been encouraged to serve the Lord with renewed vigour through a timely message on 'the fields white unto harvest.' Similarly, many a wayward soul has been brought into the shelter of the heavenly garner on hearing that, 'The harvest is past, the summer is ended, and we are not saved.'

But harvest is mainly a time of praise and thanksgiving. I can well remember how much sheer pleasure I experienced, as a boy, just from the singing of the harvest hymns.

I don't remember a single thought from any of the sermons I heard; but I do remember those lovely hymns.

Stirring hymns like, *We Plough The Fields And Scatter*, *Where Are The Reapers*, *Bringing In The Sheaves* and this one, *Come, Ye Thankful People Come*. All these bring back a flood of precious memories.

Come, Ye Thankful People Come, was first published in 1844, and its original title was *'After Harvest.'*

Only the first stanza deals with the temporal harvest here on earth. The other three portray the spiritual harvest of precious souls and the time when God shall come to 'gather in' His people.

It seems clear that this hymn is based on those encouraging words in Psalm 126:6: 'He that goeth forth and weeping, bearing precious seed, shall doubtless come again with rejoicing, bringing his sheaves with him.' The lines of each stanza are well worth a thoughtful perusal.

The author, Rev. Henry Alford DD, was born in London, England, on October 7 1810.

From all appearances he was a very godly man. Indeed, it is reported that when he was just fifteen old he dedicated himself to the Lord in the words of this sacred vow:

'I do this day, in the presence of God and my
own soul, renew my covenant with God,
and solemnly determine henceforth to
become His and to do His work as far as in
me lies.'

It seems that he never deviated from this for the rest of his life.

Biographers describe Henry Alford as a 'pious young student, an eloquent preacher, a sound Biblical critic, a man of great learning and taste, one of the most gifted men of his day, and, an affectionate man, full of good humour.'

His literary skills were displayed in every department of the art. He wrote a total of 50 books, the most important of them being his four volume Exposition of the New Testament. It took him more than twenty years to complete.

But above all, he was a superior preacher, who ever lived in the light of eternity, and sought to point his listeners heavenward.

Come ye thankful people, come,
Raise the song of harvest-home;
All is safely gathered in,
Ere the winter storms begin;
God our maker doth provide,
For our wants to be supplied;
Come to God's own temple, come,
Raise the song of harvest-home.

Count Your Blessings

Johnston Oatman

Y ou may remember an old song which Bing Crosby made popular a long time ago:
When I'm worried and can't sleep
I count my blessings, instead of sheep
And I go to sleep counting my blessings

A practical sentiment, simply put, but I think it's much better expressed in the words of Johnston Oatman's familiar hymn *Count Your Blessings*.

Johnston Oatman grew up in Lumbertown, New Jersey. His father, a local merchant, was the best singer in the state, with a rich, powerful voice. Consequently, the young lad grew up with a desire to contribute something to the faith of his father.

For a time he was a junior member of the family firm but this did not give him much opportunity for his religious ambitions. So, he studied for the Methodist ministry and, in due course, was ordained.

Again, however, the limits of one pulpit were confining and he went from church to church preaching wherever opportunity presented itself. But still he had not discovered the true calling in life.

At last, when he had reached the age of 36, he found his true talent. He concluded that since he couldn't sing like his father he would have a go at writing sacred songs for others to sing. Hopefully, he could preach to millions through his hymns.

It was 1892 when Johnston Oatman Jr. took up his pen and began to write. Titles like, *There's Not A Friend Like The Lowly Jesus, Lord, Plant My Feet On Higher Ground* and *Count Your Blessings*, are now familiar to us all.

Count Your Blessings, was written in 1897 and is regarded by many as his masterpiece. It was set to music by the composer E. O. Excell and it must be agreed that the melody suits the words perfectly.

The famous evangelist Gipsy Smith paid a glowing tribute to *Count Your Blessings*. He said, '... men sing it, boys whistle it ... and women rock their babies to sleep to it.'

Oatman wrote profusely. Some 200 hymns flowed from his pen every year, the final total topping the 5000 mark. When publishers asked him to put a price on his work it is reported that he declined to accept more than one dollar per song.

Johnston Oatman Jr died at Mount Pleasant, New Jersey, in 1936. He had found his talent; he had made his contribution ... and, through his songs, he still preaches to millions year by year.

When upon life's billows you are tempest tossed,
When you are discouraged, thinking all is lost,
Count your many blessings, name them one by one
And it will surprise you what the Lord hath done.

Are you every burdened with a load of care?
Does the cross seem heavy you are called to bear?
Count your many blessings, ev'ry doubt will fly,
And you will be singing as the days go by.

So, amid the conflict whether great or small,
Do not be discouraged, God is over all;
Count your many blessings, angels will attend
Help and comfort give you to your journey's end.

Count your blessings, name them one by one;
Count your blessings, see what God hath done;
Count your blessings, name them one by one;
And it will surprise you what the Lord hath done.

Crown Him With Many Crowns

Matthew Brides & Godfrey Thring

It is not surprising that such a magnificent opening line as *Crown Him with many crowns* should be used by different hymn-writers. But it is not known whether the two writers of this hymn ever met. Matthew Brides was one of the considerable group of Anglicans who were influenced by Newman and Faber. Godfrey Thring, a much younger man, became a Prebendary of Wells Cathedral in 1876 and it was he who altered and rearranged Bridges' hymn so that both their names now go with it in the hymn books.

But even good first lines are not always fashioned straight away. The first line of this great hymn used to be *Crown Him with crowns of gold* - a line that was for many years popular in the United States, being considered more impressive than any other description.

The five verses celebrate the kingship of Christ each with a definite theme,

Crown Him the Lord of Love
Crown Him the Son of God
Crown Him the Lord of Life
Crown Him the Lord of Peace
Crown Him the Lord of Heaven

thus making the hymn a fine example of Christian teaching about the person of Christ.

Face to Face

F. A. Beck

A pastor, his wife, and Grant Tullar had made their last call on the sick one afternoon in 1898. They hurried to the home of the pastor, wanting to have tea together before going to the evangelistic meetings that were in progress. Tullar was assisting in those services.

In their hurry to get the table spread someone failed to fill the jam dish. There was only a small bite left. The pastor and his wife knew that Tullar was very fond of the jam, so they both refused it. As the dish was passed to him, he exclaimed, 'So this is all for me, is it?' Suddenly, the thought occurred to him that 'All for Me' was a good title for a song. The little bit of jam faded into insignificance as Tullar's mind began to think on this new subject. He placed the jam dish back on the table and immediately excused himself, went to the piano and composed a melody and wrote several verses.

Before going to bed that evening, Tullar promised the pastor and his wife that he would revise the work somewhat. He never did, because the next morning the postman brought to him a letter from a lady, Mrs. Frank A. Beck. Enclosed were several poems. After reading the very first poem, he became suddenly aware that it exactly fitted the music that he had written the night before. Not a single word of the poem nor his music needed to be changed. After that, he never used his own words, but decided to use those of Mrs. Beck for the song now titled, *Face To Face*.

Face to face with Christ my Saviour,
Face to face what will it be?
When with rapture I behold Him,
Jesus Christ who died for me.

Fight The Good Fight

John Samuel Bewley Monsell

The old town of Guildford lies pleasantly on the River Wey just thirty miles from London on the road to Portsmouth.

But on April 9, 1875, a tragedy happened in the town which cast a gloom over happy Guildford. The vicar of St. Nicholas, J. S. B. Monsell, was inspecting the roof of his church, which stands guardian at the bottom of the famous High Street. Reconstruction work was going on, and the vicar was up amongst the workmen discussing their work. He missed his footing and fell heavily off the roof and died from his injuries.

He was a prolific hymn-writer. There are over three hundred to his name, but *Fight The Good Fight* is the one that has found its own niche where good hymns are sung.

Its manly, direct verses with the touch of challenge and achievement in them are a fine memorial to the Guildford vicar.

Fight the good fight with all thy might;
Christ is thy strength, and Christ thy right;
Lay hold on life, and it shall be
Thy joy and crown eternally.

Faint not, nor fear, His arms are near,
He changeth not, and thou art dear;
Only believe, and thou shalt see
That Christ is all in all to thee.

God Be With You

Jeremiah Rankin

Dr. Jeremiah Rankin, minister of the First Congregational Church in Washington D.C., wanted to write a song especially for the conclusion of Christian gatherings.

He consulted the dictionary for the definition of the word 'good-bye', and found it to be a contraction of *'God be with ye'*. Very soon the first verse was completed.

Dr. Rankin stated 'the hymn was called forth by no particular person or occasion.' It was just written for a purpose.

After completing the first verse Rankin sent the words to organist William G. Tomer of Grace Methodist Episcopal Church.

Tomer one-time school teacher, writer and clerk in the US Treasury Department, set the single verse to music and sent it back to Rankin who added a further seven verses and a chorus.

The hymn was published in the songbook *'Gospel Bells'* and taken up by the gospel singer Ira D. Sankey who introduced it on both sides of the Atlantic.

Those who can remember the famous Ulster evangelist W. P. Nicholson will recall that he always concluded his campaigns with *God Be With You* , getting the congregation to stand and wave their pocket handkerchiefs in time with the music. It's a tremendous and moving experience.

Despite its unquestionable popularity critics have torn the hymn to shreds. They point out that the line *'Till we meet,'* is repeated some forty times during a single singing.

However, it would appear that this was the intention of the author. Certainly *God Be With You*, has been a part of Christian worship all around the world for more than a century.

God be with you till we meet again,
By His counsels guide, uphold you,
With His sheep securely fold you;
God be with you till we meet again.

God be with you till we meet again,
'Neath His wings protecting hide you,
Daily manna still provide you;
God be with you till we meet again.

God be with you till we meet again,
When life's perils thick confound you;
Put His arms unfailing round you;
God be with you till we meet again.

God be with you till we meet again,
Keep love's banner floating o'er you;
Smite death's threat'ning wave before you;
God be with you till we meet again.

Till we meet, till we meet,
Till we meet at Jesus' feet
Till we meet, till we meet,
God be with you till we meet again.

God Will Take Care of You

W. Stillman Martin

In his book *Hymns of Faith*, Nathanael Olson wisely observes, 'Who can comprehend the faith and wisdom of a child?'

That's something I've often thought about myself. It seems that the faith of a child is unclouded by doubt or unbelief. Children believe implicitly in the power of God to answer prayer; and in His willingness to do so. They just can't entertain failure in the matter of their prayers.

I must add that I've often been impressed by this same simple faith in the hearts of my own children.

So it was with the nine year old son of a baptist minister in 1904.

The Rev. W. Stillman Martin had an invitation to preach in New York City. However, his wife was ill; too ill to accompany him on the journey; perhaps too ill to be left behind while he went away. He thought of cancelling the engagement and staying by her side.

Sensing his father's concern the nine year old son enquired, 'Daddy, don't you think that if God wants you to preach today, He will take care of Mother while you're away?' The father thought about this for a moment and then replied, 'Yes son, I know He will.'

Thus, assured, he kissed his wife and son goodbye and hurried of to fulfil the preaching engagement as planned.

On his return, some time later, he was pleasantly surprised to find his wife greatly improved. As he came to her bedside she handed him a poem she had written in his absence - a poem of comfort inspired by their son's simple faith.

> *Be not dismayed what'er betide,*
> *God will take care of you'*
> *Beneath his wings of love abide,*
> *God will take care of you.*

God will take care of you,
Through every day, O're all the way;
He will take care of you

The Reverend Martin placed the words on the music stand of the organ and in a short time had composed a tune which suited his wife's words perfectly.

God will take care of you is a real hymn of encouragement. It assures us that 'through days of toil, 'in times of danger or need,' in fact, 'no matter what the test,' God will take care of His people. Of course, that's a premise which is Bible based.

Thank God for the little nine year old boy who saw it more clearly than his preacher Dad did at first!

Guide Me O Thou Great Jehovah

William Williams

Each of the individual countries which go to make up these beautiful British Isles has its own personal sense of national pride.

For example, Scotland, with its majestic hills and heather, its lochs and streams and its tumbling waterfalls can be excused a certain justifiable self esteem in being called, 'The land of the mountain and the flood.'

The others, too, have their own very good reasons for this strong national pride.

I don't have time to more than mention 'Merrie England,' or my own native 'Land of saints and scholars,' although a lot could be said about both. I do want to talk about Wales, however, for that's where this hymn story takes place.

Wales is, traditionally, the land of song; and the Welsh people may well be the most enthusiastic singers in all the world. In Wales, everybody loves to sing and they sing just about everywhere.

It was always the custom for the men to sing on their way to the coalmines, although that's not done so much today. But the powerful and melodious strains of their singing still fill the air at rugby matches and other great outdoor events.

Choirs abound in every town and village and their music is popular with audiences everywhere. Wales, too, has given the world of professional singing more than its quota of national and international artistes.

In the last couple of centuries a number of great spiritual revivals have swept the land, and during these, music and singing played a major part.

Several times during those revival services the sermon was interrupted by the spontaneous outburst of congregational singing; and this was often used by the Holy Spirit to move hearts to repentance and faith in Christ Jesus.

However, not only has Wales given us singers and singing in abundance, it has also produced its fair share of hymn writers too.

One such was William Williams, a lay-preacher, who lived towards the end of the eighteenth century. At first he studied as a medical student but then decided to enter the ministry of the Church of England. However this didn't work out so he switched to open-air preaching in his native Wales.

Williams was a tireless servant of the Lord, and during the forty years of his ministry he travelled almost 100,000 miles, on foot and on horseback, preaching and singing wherever he went.

He wrote over 800 hymns, of which by far the best known is *Guide Me O Thou Great Jehovah*.

This hymn, written originally in Welsh and translated by Peter Williams, recalls some of the most trying incidents which took place during the forty year journey of the Israelites, from the bondage of Egypt, to the promised land, Canaan.

What an example to us! We too, are pilgrims, on the journey from the cradle to the grave and ultimately, to eternity. Many times our lives seem like a wilderness - 'a barren land' - as the hymn writer puts it. It is then that we must call upon the Lord to sustain us by His powerful hand.

The entire hymn is an account of God's gracious, plenteous provision for His people, at every stage of life. Surely this is one of the sources of Christian joy; to know God is with us each moment, guiding, protecting, providing.

As a result we can join with our brothers in Christ, not only in Wales, but all around the world to lift up that marvellous tune, 'Cwm Rhondda,' and say ...

> *Guide me, O thou great Jehovah,*
> *Pilgrim through this barren land;*
> *I am weak, but thou art mighty;*
> *Hold me with thy powerful hand:*
> *Bread of heaven, bread of heaven,*
> *Feed me till I want no more.*

Have Thine Own Way Lord

Adelaide Pollard

A young woman sat in a prayer meeting over eighty years ago. She was so pressed down by the weight of despair that she was hardly able to concentrate on what the speaker was saying.

Adelaide Pollard had a burden for the continent of Africa and was convinced that God wanted her to go there as a missionary. She had been on the very point of sailing away but then had to cancel everything, because the necessary funds just couldn't be raised. You can imagine her disappointment.

As she sat there the words of a prayer, often uttered by an old lady she knew, came into her thoughts: 'It's all right, Lord! It doesn't matter what you bring into our lives; just have your own way with us!'

In a moment her burden had lifted as she bowed in submission to the will of God.

Returning home that night she meditated on the story of the potter, recorded by Jeremiah:

'Then I went down to the potter's house, and, behold, he wrought a work on the wheels.

And the vessel that he made of clay was marred in the hand of the potter: so he made it again another vessel, as seemed good to the potter to make it.' Jeremiah 18:3-4.

These words seemed to fit Miss Pollard's own life and experiences exactly.

Adelaide Pollard had been born in Iowa in 1862. She had been well educated and for several years taught in a girl's school. She also had a talent for writing, both prose and poetry, and produced many religious articles, as well as a few hymns.

But her real concern was for the lost. She longed to see them reached with the message of Christ Jesus. Eventually, she began a ministry in Bible teaching and, travelling widely throughout the United States, spoke to numerous groups and churches.

Miss Pollard was also passionately interested in foreign missions. For a while she taught at the Missionary Training Institute at Nyack, New York and hoped that she would, herself, be a missionary one day. However, now it seemed that God, who had been with her all her life, was suddenly deserting her.

'But,' she thought, 'perhaps my questioning of God's will shows a flaw in my life, so God has decided to break me, as the potter broke the defective vessel, and then to mould my life again - in His own pattern,'

As she bowed in humble consecration before God, the words of a poem took shape in her mind, and she wrote:

> *Have Thine own way, Lord!*
> *Have Thine own way!*
> *Thou art the potter;*
> *I am the clay.*
> *Mould me and make me*
> *after Thy will,*
> *While I am waiting,*
> *yielded and still.*

Adelaide Pollard had learned that even Christians can be self-centred, self-possessed and self-willed. Even when doing God's work, like her planned trip to Africa, she had to be careful lest it be done in the wisdom and strength of self.

In God's own time he allowed her to go to Africa. She also spent several years in England during the first World War, returning later to her travelling ministry in the USA.

She continued to speak publicly until the age of 72 when, on her way to yet another meeting, she was taken ill in a railway station in New York City and died soon after.

The world will always have cause to be thankful for the life and ministry of that frail little woman who wrote:

> *Have Thine own way, Lord,*
> *Have Thine own way;*
> *Hold o're my being*
> *Absolute sway.*
> *Fill with Thy Spirit*
> *Till all shall see*
> *Christ only, always,*
> *Living in me.*

He The Pearly Gates Will Open

Elsie Ahlwen

In the book Hymns and Hymn Stories, Cliff Barrows relates the following story:

In preparation for a series of crusade services in Scandinavia in 1955, we were looking for something in simple Swedish to sing. Someone suggested Han skall oppna parleporten, in translation, He The Pearly Gates Will Open. Because the song is a 'natural' duet, Bev Shea graciously asked me to sing it with him. It is one of the two or three songs we sing together on rare occasions, and we have repeated it for the Danes in Copenhagen and for the American Swedes in places like Rockford, Illinois and Minneapolis, Minnesota.

Elsie Ahlwen, composer of this lovely tune, came to America form Sweden and became a student at the Moody Bible Institute. After graduation she began to work among the Swedish immigrants in Chicago, and later became a full-time evangelist. The words of this refrain had been known to her for a long time, and she often sang it to her own melody in evangelistic services throughout the country. It came to be the theme song of Elsie Ahlwen's ministry.

During a meeting in Chicago, Miss Ahlwen was approached by an old man who gave her the words for the stanzas. They had been written by Fred Blom, a former Christian worker in Sweden. Blom had come to New York early in this century, and, through circumstances that are not quite clear, had fallen into sin and was sent to prison. It was there, sick in soul and body, that he found Christ anew. The song was his expression of joy because God had 'healed his backsliding' and forgiven all his sin.

In keeping with the immigrant background of the song, it must be noted that the original was in the Swedish tongue. Not until the time of a great revival in Duluth, Minnesota was this hymn first translated into English. *He The Pearly Gates Will Open* has now been rendered in more than a dozen languages.

The hymn's message is very simple. Because of the love of God expressed in Christ our sins are forgiven, our lives are changed and we anticipate a joyful entrance into heaven. It is said that Fred Blom died in the custody of the law. While the gates of prison did not open for him, he knew that heaven's *pearly gates* would be swung wide by his Redeemer.

Elsie Ahlwen's personal testimony voices the same assurance. She had married Daniel A. Sundeen, a businessman, and they had continued a ministry together while raising their family. In 1962, they visited Chicago once again and sang *Pearly Gates* for their many friends. Shortly after Mr. Sundeen took sick and died within a week. Mrs. Sundeen wrote these words, *'It is difficult to see beyond the bend in the road where your loved one disappeared. But how good it is to know that, when my Lord calls me, the Pearly Gates will open - not because of my worthiness but because He purchased my salvation.'*

Love divine, so great and wondrous,
Deep and mighty, pure, sublime,
Coming from the heart of Jesus -
Just the same through tests of time.

He the pearly gates will open,
So that I may enter in;
For He purchased my redemption,
And forgave me all my sin.

Hold The Fort

Philip P. Bliss

Reading through this book you'll discover that there's no single formula for the writing of a successful hymn.

Some are based on a line of scripture; quite a few are the result of life's experiences; while others are just promoted by a casual remark or expression.

Nineteenth century song writer Philip P. Bliss seemed to have a penchant for this latter form.

For example, when Bliss was singing for D.L. Moody in Chicago, a great industrial exhibition was being held there.

One of the central attractions was a grand fountain. It became the rallying point for people attending the show. One would say to another 'Will you meet me at the fountain?', and the answer would come back 'Yes, that's easy to find and a beautiful place to wait.'

Bliss was struck by the words and very soon turned them to good advantage. They became the basis for a touching gospel song:

> *Will you meet me at the fountain?*
> *I shall long to have you near,*
> *When I meet my loving Saviour,*
> *When His welcome words I hear.*

He did the same kind of thing again and again.

One night in Chicago, after hearing a sermon on 'Man's love for God', Bliss reversed the theme and, while his wife prepared breakfast next morning, wrote *Jesus Loves Even Me*.

Hearing D. L. Moody tell the story of a shipwreck on Lake Eire, caused by a faulty light on the Cleveland lighthouse, he came up with *Let The Lower Lights Be Burning*.

Again, waiting for a train in Ohio, Bliss slipped into a church and hearing the preacher say, 'To be almost saved - is to be entirely lost.' *Almost Persuaded*, was the outcome.

One of his most famous compositions was written in the same way.

In October, 1864, General Sherman of the Union army poised in northwest Georgia for his celebrated 'March to the Sea.'

Some distance away, in a determined effort to hinder the progress of the Federals, General Hood and his stronger Confederate army stormed the Union encampment at Altoon Pass. The out numbered union garrison was in defeat and almost destroyed.

Then, one of its officers caught sight of a signal flag atop Kenesaw Mountain and read the encouraging message 'Hold the fort! I am coming! W.T. Sherman.'

Evangelist D.W. Whittle had been a major in Sherman's army. He recounted the events at a service in Rockford Illinois, in 1870. Bliss was the singer at the meeting and, not surprisingly, the story caught his imagination. Very soon the words and music of *Hold The Fort*, were written.

Philip P. Bliss hailed from Clearfield County, Pennsylvania. As a youth he sent one of his manuscripts to publisher George Frederick Root in Chicago, attaching a note which read, 'If my song is worth publishing I would appreciate having a flute in exchange for it.'

We're told that Root went out and bought the best flute in Chicago, dispatching it to the young musician and including the offer of a job with his publishing house, Root and Cady.

In less than 10 years the self-trained musician was directing music at Chicago's First Congregational Church and editing song books. One of them brought him $30,000 in royalties, which he promptly gave to charity.

By the time he was 32 he was the most sought after singer and composer in America. Tens of thousands thrilled to the warm sound of his beautiful baritone voice at campaigns organised by evangelists D. Whittle and D.L. Moody.

Sadly, however, his singing ministry was abruptly cut short. He and his wife were travelling on a train which crashed near Ashtabula, Ohio on December 29th 1876. Over a hundred people were burned to death in the fire which engulfed the overturned coaches. Bliss himself managed to crawl free but then fought back through the flames in an effort to rescue his wife.

All that was salvaged from the wreckage was a trunk. When it was opened there was found, among other things, a small piece of paper on which was written the lines of an unfinished hymn.

I know not what awaits me
God kindly veils my eyes ...

I wonder if they also found a flute?

Ho, my comrades! see the signal
Waving in the sky!
Reinforcements now appearing,
victory is nigh!

Hold the fort, for I am coming,
Jesus signals still;
Wave the answer back to heaven,
By Thy grace we will.

Holy, Holy, Holy

Reginald Heber

The historic hymn 'Holy, Holy, Holy' was written by Reginald Heber to be sung on Trinity Sunday in the parish of Hodnet in western England. He was vicar there in his family's church from 1807 to 1823.

Heber was an uncommon man. Born into a family of wealth and culture, he gave his life to the service of God both at home in England and far away in India. Though he possessed unusual literary gifts and was a friend of Britain's leading men of letters, his greatest ambition was to improve the hymn singing in his own church.

When Reginald Heber accepted the post of Bishop of Calcutta in 1823, it as the realisation of a longtime, deep-seated interest in foreign missions. As a bishop, Heber served a diocese that included much of the south Pacific. For three years he travelled tirelessly from place to place, using his remarkable gifts to advance the work of the church in that distant area.

On April 3rd, 1826, Heber preached on the evils of the caste system before a large audience at Trichinopoly. Afterwards, he went to cool off in the swimming pool at the home where he was staying. Some time later, he was found drowned, the result of a stroke. At the age of forty-three his brilliant life was ended, and he was buried in the Anglican church at Trichinopoly. In 1875 the Prince of Wales (later Edward VII) honoured his memory by placing a tablet there.

Reginald Heber lived and worked at a time in history when his contemporaries in English literature were becoming aware of the beauty of words and of poetic structure. The romantic movement of that day added a new dimension of elegance and lyric grace to Christian worship. This characteristic is never more evident than in Heber's hymn 'Holy, Holy, Holy' which Lord Tennyson said was the greatest in the English language.

The powerful phrases of the hymn declared the attributes of the Triune God - Father, Son and Holy Spirit. Heber shows his mastery of poetic design in composing each verse to re-emphasise the doctrine of the Trinity by using a 'trinity of words' to say something about God.

Holy, Holy, Holy! Lord God Almighty!
Early in the morning our song shall rise to Thee;
Holy, Holy, Holy! Merciful and Mighty!
God in Three Persons, blessed Trinity!

Holy, Holy, Holy! All the saints adore Thee,
Casting down their golden crowns around the glassy sea;
Cherubim and seraphim falling down before Thee,
Which wert and art, and evermore shalt be.

Holy, Holy, Holy! Tho' the darkness hide Thee,
Tho' the eye of sinful man Thy glory may not see,
Only Thou art holy; there is none beside Thee
Perfect in power, in love, and purity.

Holy, Holy, Holy! Lord God Almighty!
All Thy works shall praise Thy name, in earth, and sky and sea;
Holy, Holy, Holy! Merciful and Mighty!
God in Three Persons, blessed Trinity!

How Firm A Foundation

'K'

A lot of people seem to have the mistaken notion that Christians are somehow free from trouble and sorrow.

Perhaps some of our more popular gospel songs are responsible for this impression.

Lines like 'Jesus took my burden all away,' could well be construed to have that meaning. But what they are specifically referring to is the burden of sin and the load of guilt which the sinner bears.

However, the ordinary problems and tragedies of life which befall all men are just as much part of the lot of the believer. In fact, sometimes he may seem to have more than his share.

The metrical version of Psalm 42 records:

> *The troubles that afflict the just*
> *in number many be;*
> *But yet at length out of them all*
> *the Lord doth set him free.*

It's true, of course, that these trials perform a special function in the life of the child of God.

Paul, in Romans Ch. 5 vs 3-4 tells us that *'Tribulation worketh patience; and patience, experience, and experience, hope.'* And again in Romans Ch. 8 v 28 he advises us that *'All things work together for good.'*

There is no doubt that, just as the gold can only be brought to its full purity and value by the fire of refining, so the believer in Christ must also go through the furnace of affliction. Only thus can he be purified and made acceptable to his divine master.

The words of this hymn tell us that God uses the trials and afflictions of this world to burn up the dross of our lives; and to refine the gold.

When through fiery trials thy pathway shall lie,
My grace, all sufficient, shall be thy supply;
The flame shall not hurt thee; I only design
Thy dross to consume, and thy gold to refine.

This hymn has been a popular favourite amongst Christians ever since it first appeared, in 1787.

It was published then Dr. John Rippon, a Baptist minister in London. When it appeared in Rippon's 'A Selection of Hymns,' it was signed simply "K". All efforts to identify this mysterious "K", have been fruitless; and the mystery remains to this day.

However, there's no mystery about the message of his words. Whoever he was, he had a thorough knowledge of practical Christianity and of what is needed to encourage troubled saints in their hour of affliction.

In a hymn which draws liberally from the promises of the Bible, the author emphasises the only foundation for a faith which will prevail - the Word of God itself.

How firm a foundation, ye saints of the Lord,
Is laid for your faith in His excellent Word;
What more can He say than to you He hath said,
To you who for refuge to Jesus have fled?

How Firm A Foundation, is said to have been a particular favourite of President Andrew Jackson.

After he had left aside the burdens of the Presidency, and retired to his famous home, 'The Hermitage,' the visitors still came in their throngs, from near and far, to catch a glimpse of the great man.

The story is told that once, when the crowds were thus assembled, General Jackson called out to a local minister: 'There is a beautiful hymn on the subject of the exceeding great and precious promises of God to His people. It was a favourite with my dear wife until the day of her death. It commences thus: *'How firm a foundation, ye saints of the Lord!'* I wish you would sing now.'

And so, to please and give comfort to an aging former president, the whole assembly sang the entire hymn.

The soul that on Jesus hath leaned for repose,
I will not, I will not desert to his foes;
That soul, though all hell should endeavour to shake,
I'll never, no never, no never forsake!

How Great Thou Art

Carl Boberg

In Psalm 19, verse 1, David tells us *'The heavens declare the glory of God and the firma ment showeth his handiwork.'* This great truth is elaborated in the words of the now famous hymn *How Great Thou Art*.

It has become one of the most popular spiritual songs of our time, and I suppose could rightly be described as a Christian classic.

Although it has only become popular in the last thirty years, the origins of this hymn go back to the last century; to the majestic hills and valleys of Sweden. It was there, around 1885, that the Reverend Carl Boberg, a well known Lutheran minister wrote the original, stirring words.

Interestingly enough the Reverend Mr. Boberg's talents stretched not only to preaching and poetry. He also had political abilities for he served as a senator in the Swedish parliament for fifteen years.

In writing *How Great Thou Art*, he was 'inspired', some would say, by the natural beauty of his homeland - especially after a summer thunderstorm. Arriving home he penned three verses on the same theme and entitled this new song *O Great God*.

Over the years translations were made into German and Russian, and English; but the hymn never enjoyed the immense popularity which it does today.

However, In 1927, the Russian translation came into the hands of an English missionary couple, Mr. and Mrs. Stuart K. Hine, who were serving in the western Ukraine.

Mr. Hine sang it in Russian for a number of years and then translated three verses into English.

Surely he has vividly captured the original mood of the author with those words.

O Lord my God when I in awesome wonder,
Consider all the works Thy hands have made,
I see the stars, I hear the mighty thunder,
Thy power throughout the universe displayed,
Then sings my soul my Saviour God to Thee,
How great Thou art, how great Thou art.

When the Second World War broke out, the Hines' returned to England bringing *How Great Thou Art* with them.

A fourth verse was added in 1948, and the next year the entire hymn appeared in a gospel magazine which Mr. Hine published. It was immediately popular and soon reprints were being requested by missionaries all over the world.

The final thrust which was to give *How Great Thou Art*, the worldwide popularity it deserved came a few years later, in 1954 to be exact.

Through the good offices of Scottish publisher, Mr. Andrew Gray, a copy of Mr. Hines' leaflet came into the hands of the famous gospel singer George Beverly Shea.

It would appear that Bev. Shea fell in love with the piece immediately for he introduced it to the people of Toronto, Canada, at a crusade the next year; and then began to sing it regularly. In the New York Crusade if 1957, for example, it was sung a staggering 99 times.

No doubt the music also played a large part in making this hymn so popular with old and young. It really is something special and the simple two line melody of the beautiful tune is the perfect vehicle for those lovely words.

One verse, more than all others, sums up the gospel message superbly:

And when I think that God, His Son not sparing,
Sent Him to die, I scarce can take it in.
That on the Cross, my burden gladly bearing,
He bled and died to take away my sin.
Then sings my soul my Saviour God to thee,
How great Thou art, how great Thou art.

I Heard The Voice Of Jesus

Horatius Bonar

This hymn has been referred to as one of the most ingenious in the English language. Each stanza divides equally between invitation and response.

For example, the first verse begins with the picture of a weary soul in search of rest from the burden of sin; but concludes with the heart's glad response to the Saviour's invitation to 'Come unto me.' A similar pattern is seen running through the remaining verses.

The author, Dr. Horatius Bonar, was born in Edinburgh, Scotland, on December 19th, 1808. After his early education and ministerial studies he was ordained to the ministry of the Church of Scotland, then established, in 1837.

However, when the fateful 'disruption' took place in 1843, Bonar was one of those who separated from the established church and helped to found the Church of Scotland 'free,' or 'The Free Church' as it later came to be called.

In that same year he married Miss Jane Lundie and moved to a pastorate in Kelso, on the River Tweed, in the Scottish borders.

Their 40 years together were not without trouble and sorrow, yet they could testify that all the things that happened to them brought glory to God and gave them a wider ministry. When five of their children died early in life, Horatius wrote, 'Spare not the stroke; do with me as thou wilt; let there be naught unfinished, broken or marred, complete thy purpose that we may become thy perfect image.' Surely, the sign of true godliness.

It is reported that Dr. Bonar spent many hours each day in his study, praying aloud. A maid, who was converted in his home through these prayers, commented 'If *he* needs to pray so much, what will happen of me if *I* don't pray?'

Once when speaking to a young man about the matter of his salvation, he discovered that this individual had great difficulty in believing that the Lord could, and would save him from his sin.

Dr. Bonar asked 'Which is of greater weight - your sin, or the blood of Jesus shed for sinners?' Joyfully the young man answered 'I am sure the blood of Jesus weighs more heavily than even my sin.' Thus by the holy wisdom and devoted skill of the man of God he was brought to saving faith in Christ. Dr. Bonar firmly believed that the only antidote to crimson sin is the cleansing blood of the Lord Jesus.

He was a prolific writer, editing two magazines, publishing many articles and producing hundreds of tracts. One of these, entitled *Believe and live*, and said to be a favourite of Queen Victoria, sold a million copies. He also wrote 600 hymns and translated at least 60 Psalms.

Bonar was a man with a powerful and consecrated intellect, a deep knowledge of the Scriptures, and a physical stature both tall and strong. But these somewhat overpowering characteristics were offset by a gentle, sympathetic nature and a childlike faith.

Perhaps it was the childlikeness which gave him such a love for little ones. Certainly it was his love and concern for the young that led him to the writing of his hymns.

When he observed their rather indifferent spirit towards the traditional singing of the Psalms; but a much livelier attitude when singing their weekday songs, he decided to write sacred words for their joyful tunes.

The experiment met with instant success and brought excellent results too. One woman who had attended his weekly Bible class later testified, 'We still cherish the hymn he wrote specially for us.' It ran ;

> *Shall this life of mine be wasted,*
> *Shall this vineyard lie untilled?*
> *Then no longer idly dreaming,*
> *Shall I fling my years away;*
> *But, each precious hour redeeming,*
> *Wait for the eternal day.*

In 1866 Horatius Bonar moved to Edinburgh, the city of his birth. There he continued his faithful labours for the Master until his death on July 31st, 1889. A sad loss to Scotland, its church and its people, but a life lived to the service of others and the glory of God.

I heard the voice of Jesus say,
'Come unto me and rest;
Lay down, thou weary one, lay down
Thy head upon my breast.'

I came to Jesus as I was
Weary, and worn, and sad;
I found in him a resting place,
And he has made me glad.

I Need Thee Every Hour

Annie S. Hawks

Several of the hymn stories in this book relate the trying experiences of the children of God and how their afflictions have been the material from which great hymns were written.

However, here's one which came into being through completely different and happier circumstances. It makes a refreshing and interesting change.

Annie Sherwood Hawks was born in Hoosick, New York, on 28th May 1835. Even from an early age she was writing poetry and, at 14, had some published in a newspaper.

When she married, at 24, she moved to live in the Brooklyn area of New York. There, she and her husband joined the church whose pastor was the noted hymn writer and composer, Dr. Robert S. Lowry.

Dr. Lowry immediately recognised Mrs Hawks talent for writing and encouraged her to use it. In fact he even offered her a challenge. 'If you'll write the words,' he said, 'I'll write the music,' and he was as good as his word.

I Need Thee Every Hour, was written in April 1872 and is thought to have been based on the exhortation of Jesus in John 15 verses 4 and 5.

'Abide in me, and I in you. As the
branch cannot bear fruit of itself,
except it abide in the vine; no more can
ye, except ye abide in me. I am the
vine, ye are the branches: he that
abideth in me, I am in him, the same
bringeth forth much fruit: for without
me ye can do nothing.'

The new hymn was first performed in November that year at the National Sunday School Convention in Cincinatti, Ohio. Very soon it was taken up by the famous evangelistic team of Moody and Sankey, who, it seems likely, did most to make it popular. It was translated into many other languages too; and even featured in the great Chicago World's Fair.

But what about the actual penning of those comforting lines?

Well, a short time before her death, on January 3rd 1918, Mrs Hawkes gave the full background story. I quote her own words.

'I remember well the circumstances under which I wrote the hymn. It was a bright June day, and I became so filled with the sense of the nearness of my Master that I began to wonder how anyone could live without Him, in either joy or pain. Suddenly, the words I need Thee every hour, flashed into my mind, and very quickly the thought had full possession of me.

Seating myself by the open windows, I caught up my pencil and committed the words to paper - almost as they are today. A few months later Dr. Robert Lowry composed the tune *Need*, for my hymn and also added the refrain.

For myself, the hymn, at its writing, was prophetic rather than expressive of my own experiences, for it was wafted out to the world on the wings of love and joy, instead of under the stress of great personal sorrow, with which it has often been associated.

At first I did not understand why the hymn so greatly touched the throbbing heart of humanity. Years later, however, under the shadow of a great loss, I came to understand something of the comforting power of the words I had been permitted to give out to others in my hours of sweet serenity and peace.'

It must have given the talented lady great satisfaction to write something which has been such a blessing to so many.

I need Thee every hour,
Most gracious Lord;
No tender voice like Thine,
Can peace afford.

I need Thee, O I need Thee!
Every hour I need Thee:
O bless me now my Saviour!
I come to Thee.

In Heavenly Love Abiding

Anna Laetitia Waring

One of the surprises about devotional verse of the mid-nineteenth century is the way in which it sold. Edition after edition of verse by writers who would not be accounted poets in the strict sense were bought up. Anna L. Waring's poems had that welcoming experience. At the age of thirty in 1850 she published her *Hymns and Meditations*, a small book of nineteen hymns which by 1863 had gone into ten editions, and contained thirty-eight hymns.

A Glamorganshire Welsh woman, her poems have the phrase and turn of one who not only had a genuine piety but knew how to express it. Four of her hymns have found permanent recognition: *My Heart Is Resting O My God, Go Not Far From me O My Strength, Father I Know That All My Life* and *In Heavenly Love Abiding*.

The nineteenth century would have voted for the first named as her best hymn, but the twentieth, judging by the popularity of its choice, goes for *In heavenly love abiding*. Not a robust or a bold hymn of discipleship, but one of calm and complete gospel assurance.

> *Wherever He may guide me,*
> *No wants shall turn me back;*
> *My Shepherd is beside me,*
> *And nothing can I lack:*
>
> *His wisdom ever waketh,*
> *His sight is never dim;*
> *He knows the way He taketh,*
> *And I will walk with Him.*

In My Heart There Rings A Melody

Elton Menno Roth

Not many people are blessed with a fine singing voice. Others can't even sing in tune. My father had neither a good singing voice nor could he carry a tune. He was what you might call 'tone deaf.' Yet he loved music and enjoyed listening to it.

Nothing gave him more pleasure than to sit while my mother played the piano and rattled off the familiar songs and hymns; always concluding with his favourite Scottish air *The Road To The Isles.*

As I said, he didn't have much success in keeping a tune, but with one exception. *In My Heart There Rings A Melody.* For some reason this is one spiritual song he was able to sing right through, note perfect, and I remember him singing it many, many times.

Perhaps that was because he, as this song states, had 'the melody' in his own heart.

In the fortieth Psalm the psalmist testified: *'He hath put a new song in my mouth, even praise unto our God.'*

This new song doesn't have to have either melody, harmony or rhythm! It's the song of the heart. The song of love; the song of joy; the song of peace and serenity which comes through knowing Jesus as Saviour.

Someone has said 'If there were more singing Christians, there would be more Christians!' If this heart song of love, joy and peace is evident in our lives every day it will make us conspicuous to all around us. As the Psalmist pointed out in the previously quoted passage 'Many shall see it, and fear, and shall trust in the Lord.'

In My Heart There Rings A Melody, was written by Elton Menno Roth. For many years he was a distinguished church musician; singing, composing and conducting. In fact, after studying under several prominent teachers, he organised a number of professional choirs in the 1930's and these achieved recognition throughout the USA in their concert tours.

Mr. Roth explained that this hymn was written while he was conducting an evangelistic meeting in Texas. He recalled the incident thus:

'One hot summer afternoon I took a little walk to the cotton mill just outside of town. On my way back through the burning streets of this typical plantation village, I became weary with the oppressive heat, and paused at a church on the corner.

The door being open, I went in. There were no people in the pews, no minister in the pulpit. Everything was quiet, with a lingering sacred presence. I walked up and down the aisle and began singing *'In my heart there rings a melody'* then hurried into the pastor's study to find some writing paper. I drew a staff and sketched the melody, remaining there for an hour or more to finish the song, both words and music.

That evening I introduced it by having over two hundred boys and girls sing it at the open air meeting, after which the audience joined in the singing. I was thrilled as it seemed my whole being was transformed into song!'

In every aspect of the Lord's work it's important that we give Him the best. Too many people seem to be quite content to offer their Lord anything, regardless of how shoddy, unrehearsed or amateur it is.

This is wrong! We ought to give the Lord the very best we can. However, far above this consideration there's the importance of remembering that God is more concerned with whether or not we have a song in our heart. It's this melody of life which makes us different from the crowd and will convince others that salvation is real.

I have a song that Jesus gave me,
It was sent from heaven above;
There never was a sweeter melody,
'Tis the melody of love.

In my heart there rings a melody,
There rings a melody ...
with heaven's harmony;
In my heart there rings a melody;
There rings a melody of love.

In The Garden

C. Austin Miles

This is more than a hymn with pleasant phrases about gardens and birds and roses. C. Austin Miles, the composer, gives us the clue himself.

'One day in March, 1912, I was seated in the darkroom where I kept my photographic equipment and organ. I drew my Bible toward me; it opened at my favourite chapter, John 20 ... That meeting of Jesus and Mary had lost none of its power to charm.

As I read it that day, I seemed to be part of the scene. I became a silent witness to that dramatic moment in Mary's life, when she knelt before her Lord, and cried, 'Rabboni' ... Under the inspiration of this vision I wrote as quickly as the words could be formed the poem exactly as it has since appeared. That same evening I wrote the music.'

The specific reference to a garden becomes much clearer when we learn that C. Austin Miles was writing about the first Easter morning and the garden in which Jesus was buried. It was here Mary Magdalene came alone very early, 'while the dew was still on the roses.' When Jesus first spoke to her, she thought it was the gardener; but when He called her by name, she recognised His voice.

It is difficult to imagine what Mary's feelings and actions were at that moment. She had seen Jesus die on the cross. She was now coming to anoint His dead body with spices.But there He was, standing before her and talking to her. He was alive! She may have been startled at first, but when His identity became clear, she was filled with joy - as the song says, like a melody ringing in her heart!

No doubt Mary wanted nothing more than to stay there in the garden with Jesus, but He ordered her to go and tell His disciples what had happened.

Mary's experience is relived by every person who confronts the risen Christ and realises His presence in the routine of daily life. We too can 'walk and talk' with Christ and be assured that we belong to Him. This experience is very real to a believer and brings a joy that is beyond any other satisfaction. Indeed, it may sometimes seem that no one else has ever known as much delight as we experience, walking each day with Christ. At least, this was author Miles' conviction when he wrote:

> I come to the garden alone,
> While the dew is still on the roses;
> And the voice I hear, falling on my ear,
> The Son of God discloses.
>
> He speaks, and the sound of His voice
> Is so sweet the birds hush their singing,
> And the melody that He gave to me,
> Within my heart is ringing!
>
> I'd stay in the garden with Him
> Though the night around me be falling,
> But He bids me go; through the voice of woe,
> His voice to me is calling.
>
> And He walks with me, and He talks with me,
> And He tells me I am His own,
> And the joy we share as we tarry there,
> None other has ever known.

It Is Well With My Soul

Horatio G. Spafford

Unclouded skies and gentle winds do nothing to test our vessel of faith. It takes the storm and tempest to prove the strength of our trust in the Almighty.

The prophet Isaiah records that, God keeps in perfect peace all who trust in Him. (Isa. 26. 3).

Nowhere is this truth more aptly illustrated than in the story which accompanies the writing of the hymn It Is Well With My Soul.

Horatio G. Spafford lived, with his wife and four daughters, in Chicago. He was a lawyer by profession and a devout and sincere Christian.

One day in 1873 he stood on the quayside in Chicago and bid farewell to his family as they set sail to visit relatives in far off Europe He was not to realise that he would never see most of them again.

Some days later their ship, bound for Le Havre in France collided with another steamship in mid-Atlantic, and sank almost immediately.

Before it did so, however, Mrs Spafford was able to have a prayer with her children and commit them to the mercy of the Lord. That was the last time she would ever see them on this earth.

Fortunately, a lifeboat spotted Mrs Spafford and she was rescued. When she arrived in Britain, with the rest of the survivors, she sent her husband this terse, but telling message: 'SAVED ALONE.'

The words struck Horatio Spafford with full force, and, understandably, plunged him into deep sorrow. He left for England, without delay, to comfort his grief-stricken wife.

The great American evangelist D.L. Moody and his associate, singer Ira D. Sankey, were conducting a campaign in Edinburgh at the time. They were personal friends of the Spaffords and came down to London to give whatever help and comfort they could. They found their friends in surprisingly good spirits, strong in faith and able to say through their tears, 'It is well; the will of God be done.'

Three years after that tragedy, Mr. Spafford wrote his hymn *It Is Well With My Soul*, in memory of his four precious daughters. Happily each of them had personally received Jesus Christ as Saviour before embarking on that fateful voyage.

It would be very difficult for any of us to predict how we would react under circumstances similar to those experienced by the Spaffords. But we do know that the God who sustained them would also be with us.

No matter what circumstances overtake us may we be able to say with Horatio Spafford

> *When peace like a river, attendeth my way,*
> *When sorrows like sea billows roll;*
> *Whatever my lot, Thou hast taught me to say,*
> *It is well, it is well with my soul.*

> *Though Satan should buffet, though trials should come,*
> *Let this blest assurance control,*
> *That Christ hath regarded my helpless estate,*
> *And hath shed His own blood fro my soul!*

> *It is well ... with my soul!*
> *It is well, it is well, with my soul.*

I Think When I Read That Sweet Story

Jemima Thompson

Like quite a number of the other hymns we have considered, this one began life very humbly - on the back of an envelope! That was away back in 1841, and it happened like this.

The author, Jemima Thompson, had been spending some time at an infant school gaining knowledge of the system.

As the teacher and children marched around the classroom, Miss Thompson was intrigued by the melody of the tune they kept time to. It turned out to be a Greek air called *Salamis*, and immediately a search began to find appropriate words for this beautiful music. However, although several hymnals were consulted, no suitable words could be found.

Sometime later, while riding alone on a stagecoach, Jemima began to hum the haunting melody again. Suddenly, the words we are now so familiar with, began to form in her heart and mind, and, taking an envelope from her bag she quickly jotted them down.

Very soon she taught the new words to her school children; and the following Sunday they sang them in Miss Thompson's father's church. The Reverend Thompson was delighted at the sound and when he asked who had written the lovely words was met with a chorus of little voices all saying 'Jemima did'.

Next day he sent the words off to *The Sunday School Teacher's Magazine,* and they were printed right away. From there, the popularity of the new hymn grew by leaps and bounds. It's success was guaranteed.

Jemima Thompson was born near London, England on August 19th 1813. She came to the Saviour at the very tender age of ten and by the time she was thirteen was already writing for a periodical called *The Juvenile Magazine.*

Later, she edited the first ever missionary magazine for children and included contributions from such famous missionary names as David Livingstone, James Moffat, and James Montgomery.

Jemima herself had plans to go to India as a missionary to women, but ill heath prevented her from ever setting sail.

In 1834 she married the Reverend Samuel Luke, a congregational minister, and devoted herself to her duties as 'lady of the manse,' as well as to further writing.

However, it is for this one great hymn that she is best known. It is probably true to say that by means of it she has reached multitudes of the Lord and has inspired many more to answer God's call to service on the mission field.

Jemima Thompson Luke finally said farewell to this world in 1906 at the ripe old age of 93. Her earthly ministry was ended but her memory will live on forever in the words of her beautiful hymn.

I think when I read that sweet story of old,
When Jesus was here among men,
How He called little children as lambs to his fold,
I should like to have been with Him then.

I wish that His hands had been placed on my head,
That His arm had been thrown around men,
And that I might have seen His kind look when He said,
'Let the little ones come unto Me'

Ivory Palaces

Henry Barraclough

The famous gospel song *Ivory Palaces* was written in the mountains of North Carolina. In the summer of 1915 the famous evangelist Dr. J. Wilbur Chapman was preaching at the Presbyterian conference grounds at Montreat. With him were the songleader Charles M. Alexander, soloist Albert Brown, and their pianist Henry Barraclough. Barraclough, the author of this hymn, was a twenty-four-year-old Britisher; he had met Chapman the previous year during a preaching mission in England.

During the conference, the evangelist spoke one evening on the forty-fifth Psalm.

He believed, that this is a prophetic, 'Messianic' psalm which speaks of the relationship of Christ, the bridegroom, to His bride, the Church.

The eighth verse of the psalm was Dr. Chapman's text:

'All thy garments smell of myrrh, and aloes, and cassia, out of the ivory palaces, whereby they have made thee glad.'

The oriental spices and perfumes mentioned here were used for many purposes. They were often poured on clothing so that their delightful odour seemed to be part of the very texture of the cloth. Following the suggestions of these provocative phrases, Dr. Chapman developed his sermon on the symbolism of the perfumed garments of an oriental bridegroom.

'Myrrh' was an exotic perfume associated with ecstasy and joy; it represents the beauty of the person of Christ - that beauty which attracts us to Him. 'Aloes' was a bitter herb used in embalming, which should remind us that our Lord had many sorrows during His lifetime, culminating in a shameful and painful death on the cross. 'Cassia' was a spicy perfume that was also a medication; Jesus Christ is like a potion that heals us from the wounds of sin when we look to Him in repentance.

After the evening service, 'Charlie' Alexander and Henry Barraclough drove some friends to the Blue Ridge YMCA Hostel a few miles away. Sitting in the front seat of the car, young Barraclough thought about the message and the four short phrases of the refrain began to take shape in his mind. When they stopped at a little village store, he quickly wrote them down on a 'visiting card' - the only paper that was available. Returning to the conference hotel, he worked out the first three using the outline of Chapman's message. The following morning Mrs. Alexander and Mr. Brown sang the new hymn in the Montreat conference centre.

Later, Dr. Chapman suggested that Barraclough add a fourth verse, reminding us that one day Christ will come again wearing the same glorious garments. I believe that through all eternity we will be reminded of the beauty of our Lord, of His suffering for us, and of the forgiveness and cleansing which He has made possible.

Out of the ivory palaces,
Into a world of woe,
Only His great, eternal love
Made my Saviour go.

Jesus Lover Of My Soul

Charles Wesley

No study of the great hymns of the Christian faith would be complete without considering the work of the one man who did more for English hymns than any other - Charles Wesley.

Even though his father was a clergyman, Charles Wesley grew up without ever coming to a knowledge of sins forgiven or the assurance of salvation. Thankfully however, like his famous brother John, he finally found spiritual peace through the help of the Moravians, especially that of Peter Bohler, who explained to him the nature of justification by faith alone.

Thus it was that on Whit Sunday, May 21st 1738, Charles Wesley found peace with God through our Lord Jesus Christ.

From that time he was as much on fire to preach the gospel as his brother; and equally bold and tireless in doing so. Above all, he translated the gospel message into song, furnishing both a powerful means of evangelism and a rich reservoir of devotion.

On the first anniversary of his conversion he wrote those majestic lines:-

O for a thousand tongues to sing
My great Redeemer's praise,
The glories of my God and King,
The triumphs of His grace!

These lines have been used to open successive editions of the Methodist hymn book ever since.

Hymn writing came easily to Charles Wesley, anytime, anywhere, so that from his busy pen there flowed some nine thousand sacred songs.

Christendom still sings many of them. Composition like *Love Divine All Loves Excelling, Christ The Lord Is Risen Today,* and *Hark The Herald Angels Sing,* are still firm favourites with believers all around the globe.

Just now we are considering one of the most popular and beautiful of all hymns *Jesus Lover Of My Soul,* written just two years after Charles Wesley came to know the Lord as his Saviour.

Strange as it may seem, it wasn't given a place in any Methodist hymnal until nine years later after the author's death. It is said that his brother John thought it much too sentimental to be used as a spiritual song.

No one is really sure what experience prompted the writing of the lovely words, but it seems certain that something did.

Some say that a little bird flew into Wesley's room for protection and then sought refuge inside the folds of his coat, thus giving him the idea of believer's flying to the Lord's bosom for their protection.

But whatever did, or did not happen, Charles Wesley's prayer-poem has found a responsive chord in the ears and hearts of tens of thousands.

Jesus, Lover of my soul,
Let me to Thy bosom fly,
While the nearer waters roll,
While the tempest still is high:
Hide me, O my Saviour, hide,
Till the storm of life is past;
Safe into the haven guide,
O receive my soul at last!

Plenteous grace with Thee is found,
Grace to cover all my sin;
Let the healing streams abound,
Make and keep me pure within:
Thou of life the Fountain art,
Freely let me take of Thee,
Spring Thou up within my heart,
Rise to all eternity.

Jesus Loves Me

Susan and Anna Warner

One of the most delightful things for any minister is to have a congregation with plenty of children and young people.

What life - and laughter - and fun they bring about the place! They seem to be always happy; they're so full of excitement; and - *they're nearly always good!*

I like their cute little faces, their wide excited eyes and their simple, trusting ways. I like their singing too. There's something very special about the lisping, lilting voices of children that touches the heart.

Of course the hymn which is most closely associated with children is *Jesus Loves Me.*

It was written in 1859 by Susan and Anna Warner who were the daughters of a New York lawyer. The two young women were talented writers and in 1859 published a novel entitled *Say and Seal.* It became a best seller.

However, even the very best of novels remain popular for only a limited time, and *Say and Seal,* was no exception. Eventually it went the way of all the others.

But as long as *Jesus Loves Me,* is still sung by children it will never be entirely forgotten. As a poem it first appeared within the pages of the Warner girls' novel.

In the story, two of the characters, Faith Derrick and John Endecott Linden are greatly concerned for a very sick little fellow named Johnny Fax.

Johnny's condition becomes critical and, in his misery, he asks Mr Linden, who was also the Sunday School teacher, to take him in his strong arms and comfort him. Mr. Linden readily does so and, picking up the feverish boy, walks slowly back and forth across the room trying to console him.

Suddenly, Johnny pleads 'Sing!'

As Faith listens she hears John Linden sing a beautiful song which neither she nor Johnny has heard before.

Jesus loves me! this I know,
For the Bible tells me so,
Little ones to Him belong,
They are weak, but He is strong.

With this he sought to comfort the final moments of the dying lad. Indeed, a few hours later, little Johnny Fax went to be with the one who loved him so much.

The lines of the poem came to the attention of the famous composer William Bradbury, and in 1861 he set them to music and added the chorus...

Yes Jesus loves me! yes Jesus loves me!
Yes Jesus loves me! the Bible tells me so.

Jesus Saviour Pilot Me

Edward Hopper

Four and a half of the most happy years of my life were spent as the minister of a church in Kilkeel, County Down.

Kilkeel, among other things, is home for the largest fishing fleet in Ulster, so perhaps it's no surprise that, while there, I developed a passion for the sea.

I used to go down to the harbour many an evening, to watch the boats unloading their catch and listen to the auctioneers, as the harvest of the sea was turned into money.

On a few occasions I enjoyed the added privilege of going out on a trawler for a day and soon learned quite a bit about charts and navigation, searching for, and finding fish, and 'shooting' and 'hauling', nets. I even tried my hand at gutting the fish but decided I would never become an expert.

Those who put to sea for a living follow a hazardous and dangerous occupation. It's my opinion that they earn every penny they get.

If you've ever stood on the shore, on a stormy day, and watched the boats disappear behind the waves and then reappear again, you'll know what I mean. If you've ever sailed in those conditions you'll have cause to know!

No wonder the Psalmist was guided to write:

'They that go down to the sea in ships, that do business in great waters; these see the works of the Lord, and his wonders in the deep. For he commandeth, and raiseth the stormy wind, which lifteth up the waves thereof. They mount up to the heaven, they go down again to the depths: their soul is melted because of trouble. They reel to and fro, and stagger like a drunken man, and are at their wit's end.'

(Psalm 107: 23-27)

The sailor's plight, and need, is well summed up in the words of Edward Hopper's hymn:

Jesus Saviour, pilot me
Over life's tempestuous sea;
Unknown waves before me roll,
Hiding rock and treacherous shoal;
Chart and compass come from Thee,
Jesus, Savour, pilot me.

Like many another person with a love for the sea, Edward Hopper was a town man by birth.

After completing his education in his native city of New York he held pastorates in Greenville N.Y., and Sag Harbour, Long Island. Then came the invitation to New York Harbour's 'Church of the Sea and Land', where he ministered every week to a congregation made up largely of sailors.

After the fashion of Methodist hymn-writer, Charles Wesley, who often wrote to suit his congregations, Hopper composed for the men who put to sea in ships. His compositions include *They Pray The Best Who Pray And Watch* and *Wrecked And Struggling In Mid-Ocean*, hardly titles to catch the imagination.

However, his most famous composition has been taken to the hearts of the people everywhere.

Jesus Saviour, Pilot Me, was first published in 1871, in The Sailor's Magazine. Philadelphia composer, John Edgar Gould, set it to music the night before he left for Algiers on a trip for the betterment of his health.

In fact he never returned and the sailors were left to mourn the man who had put music to Edward Hopper's lovely hymn.

However, at the time, none of Hopper's congregation knew that the minister was the author of such a masterpiece. *Jesus Saviour Pilot Me*, had been in circulation for nine years before Hopper's name became associated with it. He always kept the secret of his hymn-writing talent to himself. Nobody knew how many hymns he had written, for even when he did sing them he often used fictitious names.

On April 23rd 1888, Edward Hopper settled back in an easy chair. He was 72 years old and suffering from a weak heart. Still, he felt strong enough to write and so began outlining a new hymn.

When they found him he was still seated in his chair with the pencil in his hand. The sheet of paper had drifted to the floor and on it was the title of the new composition *Heaven*. But Edward Hopper was already there!

Jesus The Very Thought Of Thee

Bernard of Clairvaux

Hymns often raise odd associations in the mind. This hymn written by Bernard of Clairvaux, always takes me to the green, mountainous country beyond Grenoble in France and to, La Grande Chartreuse. Its secluded position in the mountains makes it a remote spot even today, but nothing to what it was in the spring of 1125 when Bernard came riding up the ravines to visit it.

Bernard's letters had already made him famous, but his hosts were disappointed to see him riding such a splendid horse and sitting on so fine a saddle. It was mentioned to Bernard, who was surprised at the criticism. Although he had ridden miles on it he had not noticed, he said, how fine the saddle was, and in any case the horse was not his: it had been lent to him for the journey by his uncle!

His friends were happy again, and marvelled at Bernard's deep contemplation which had hidden from him what they saw at first glance. He was later riding by the lake of Geneva, and his companion asked him what he thought of the lake. 'What lake?' asked Bernard.

Few in Christian history was more deeply devoted to Jesus in every thought and action than Bernard of Clairvaux.

Seven centuries afterwards David Livingstone wrote in his African journal, 'The hymn of St. Bernard on the name of Christ pleases me so; it rings in my ears as I wonder across the wide, wide wilderness."

Jesus, the very thought of Thee
With sweetness fills the breast;
But sweeter far Thy face to see,
And in Thy presence rest.

Jesus Thy Blood And Righteousness

Nicholas L.V. Zinzendorf

The family of Count Nicholas Ludvig Von Zinzendorf was one of the wealthiest in all Saxony. So when the young nobleman wound up his law studies in the university of Wittenberg he set out to see the world in luxury.

However, he only got as far as an art gallery in Dusseldorf. There, pondering a painting of Christ with his bowed head and the inscription 'This have I done for thee, and what hast thou done for me''', the young count was smitten with conviction.

He went back to his estate in Berthelsdorf with a heavy heart - and miserable. But God was dealing with him. At twenty-two, on his wedding day, he and his bride put aside their rank of nobility to follow in the simple footsteps of the lowly man of Galilee.

Shortly after this a religious outcast named Christian David wandered into Berthelsdorf. Christian David belonged to a society known as 'The Moravian Brethren'. The Moravians had been founded some three hundred years earlier by John Huss, known in history books as 'The Old Goose of Bohemia.' Zinzendorf took David in and then rounded up all the other brethren he could find so that within ten years, six hundred Moravians were living on his estate. He organised them into missionary groups and sent them off to the far corners of the earth.

To Greenland they went, to Holland and India, to America and the Indies these pioneers of missionary endeavour set forth with holy zeal.

Long before William Carey put down his cobbler's last to take up the Bible and long before John and Charles Wesley had preached a sermon or wrote a hymn, the Moravians had one hundred and sixty-five missions scattered throughout the world.

They faced disease, poverty, loneliness and persecution; but nothing stopped them from carrying on the work of the crucified Christ, whose picture their leader had seen in an art gallery at Dusseldorf.

On December 21st 1741, Zinzendorf himself founded a mission and preached to the Indians in Pennsylvania. As it was only four days to Christmas he named the colony Bethlehem. It's a great steel centre today and the Moravian capital of the United States.

The former Count *saw* the world - but not in luxury. When he died, back in his native Saxony, aged sixty, there wasn't even enough money to pay for his grave.

Zinzendorf wrote 2,000 hymns during his long life of service for Christ, among them this one penned in 1739 while on board a ship on the way to establish a mission in the West Indies.

> *Jesus: Thy blood and righteousness,*
> *My beauty are, my glorious dress,*
> *'Midst flaming words, in these arrayed;*
> *With joy shall I lift up my head.*

When you think of all that Count Zinzendorf gave up and all he endured for the sake of Christ's kingdom surely you're bound to be persuaded that he meant everything he wrote.

Just As I Am

Charlotte Elliott

I t must be true to say that no sacred song or hymn has been more used to bring sinners to the feet of Jesus, than this one.

Sung by grand choirs in vast crusades as hundreds have come or by congregations, large and small, as one's and two's have come; this hymn has moved the hearts of multitudes.

Just As I Am, rings with a clear, positive note. It invites the sinner, just as he is, with all his sin, in all his unworthiness, despite his fears, though poor, wretched and blind, to come to the Saviour.

That's an invitation which is absolutely scriptural! We don't need to wait until our lives have been straightened out before we come to Christ. There's nothing we can do which will ever make us more acceptable in God's sight. The Bible clearly teaches that God loves the sinner, just the way he is, and wants him to come like that.

Only Jesus Christ can deliver us from the guilt and penalty of sin. Only He can solve all the problems of life. Only He can give us peace and joy and hope for the future. It was out of her feelings of frustration and hopelessness that the daughter of an Anglican minister in Brighton, England, wrote the words of this fine hymn.

One day in 1833, when Charlotte Elliott was in her forty-fourth year, she was feeling unusually depressed and alone. The other members of her family had gone off to a church function while she, an invalid and bedridden, remained at home.

Before her illness she had lived a happy, carefree life enjoying its many pleasures and gaining a measure of popularity, as a portrait artist.

Now, all of this past and stricken with the sickness which was to plague her for the rest of her life, she felt utterly useless and cut off. In addition, although she had been a Christian for many years, she began to have doubts about her relationship with the Lord. How could she be sure that all was well with her soul?

In her distress she began to list scriptural reasons for believing that she was, indeed, a child of God. She recognised the power of the Saviour's precious blood. She remembered His promise to receive all who come to Him by faith; and His ability to pardon, cleanse and save.

As she meditated on these great truths her heart was warmed and very soon Charlotte Elliott, who was also fond of writing poetry, was putting down her thoughts in verse:

Just as I am, without one plea,
but that Thy blood was shed for me,
And that Thou bidst me come to Thee,
O Lamb of God, I come, I come.

It's just here that we encounter a new slant to the story.

Charlotte Elliott's brother was anxious to start a school to benefit the children of poor clergymen, and had organised a bazaar to raise funds.

It seemed that everybody in the town had helped with the project. Everybody, that is, except Charlotte, who was so stricken with paralysis that she could barely drag herself around her room.

So she published her new poem *Just As I Am*, in the hope that from its sale she could contribute something to her brother's school fund.

The poem was instantly successful and was soon selling all over England in large numbers as well as being translated into a number of foreign languages.

Charlotte Elliott never did enjoy good heath for the rest of her life. She remained bedridden until the Lord, at last, called her home when she was eighty-two years old.

However, before her death she received more than a thousand letters of thanks and compliments from people who were grateful that she had written *Just As I Am*.

Just as I am, Thou wilt receive,
Wilt welcome, pardon, cleanse, relieve;
Because Thy promise I believe,
O Lamb of God, I come, I come.

Leaning On The Everlasting Arms

Elisha A. Hoffman

There was a time in America when only those who could afford private lessons were able to sing by music. There were few songbooks, and church-goers depended on songleaders to set the tune of the hymn and call out the words, line by line, while the congregations sang after them. The same practice is still followed in the highlands of Scotland to this day at funerals and on certain other occasions.

But back to our American story.

Through the persistent representations of a musician called Lowell Mason music became an official subject in the schools. Songbooks were published and trained music-masters were sent into rural America to teach the people how to sing.

Professor A.J. Showalter was one such music-master.

One day in 1887, after music class had been dismissed, he collected his books, locked up the church house where they met and made his way across town to the boarding house where he had put up for his brief stay in Hartselle, Alabama.

When he arrived, two letters from former students in South Carolina were waiting for him.

Showalter read the first letter. It bought the sad news that this student had just recently and suddenly lost his wife. The professor left the letter aside and decided to answer it later.

Opening the second one he found that it brought news identical to that of the first. What a tragic coincidence! Two former students had each been plunged into tragedy, through the same circumstances, and on the same day.

In an effort to console his two young friends Showalter wrote: *'The eternal God is thy refuge and underneath are the everlasting arms'*. He paused, and put down his pen.

In that single line of Scripture lay the theme of a great hymn. His pupils could read music, and they could sing - for he had taught them. Then why not write them a *song* of comfort instead of a letter? Quickly he wrote the chorus:

> *Leaning, leaning, safe and secure from all alarms,*
> *Leaning, leaning, leaning on the everlasting arms.*

Professor Showalter sent the chorus off to the Rev. Elisha Hoffman in Pennsylvania, and Hoffman - himself the author of over 2,000 hymns, very soon produced three beautiful verses.

When Showalter received Hoffman's finished work he wrote the music for it and another great hymn was born.

We don't have any record of what effect the song message had on those for whom it was written but we do know it has been a great blessing to thousands ever since.

> *What have I to dread, what have I to fear,*
> *Leaning on the everlasting arms?*
> *I have blessed peace with my Lord so near,*
> *Leaning on the everlasting arms.*

Let The Lower Lights
Be Burning

Philip P. Bliss

I love the sea! I love boats! Nothing gives me more pleasure than to take my own little boat down to the water and spend a few hours just pottering about.

One of my favourite sailing spots is the beautiful area of Carlingford Lough in County Down, where the air is bracing and the scenery majestic. But the tides there are strong and the currents can be very treacherous. You really do need to know what you are doing and, perhaps more important, where you are going.

I was very fortunate, then, that a good friend of mine, who is also a keen sailor, went with me when I first ventured onto Carlingford. Harry came to show me the way around and to point out 'the marks', as they call them.

To put it in 'land-lubbers' language he had come with me to point out the navigation marks. His knowledge of the area, gained from years of sailing there, was invaluable. The few hours he spent with me that day, sailing from Greencastle, over to Carlingford harbour, down by the Block House and out as far as the lighthouse at Cranfield, were greatly appreciated.

I can now sail that stretch of water with complete confidence, because I know the danger spots and how to stay clear of them.

How important it is to be able to find your way, especially in treacherous circumstances. That's what D.L. Moody must have had in mind when he told the following story:

On a dark and stormy night in the last century, when the waves rolled like mountains and not a single star lit the darkness of the sky, a large passenger ship cautiously edged it way towards the harbour at Cleveland, Ohio. On board, the pilot knew that, on such a night, he could only find the safety of the harbour by keeping the two lower shore lights in line with the main beacon.

'Are you sure this is Cleveland?' asked the captain, who could see only one light, that from the lighthouse.

'Yes, I'm quite sure,' relied the pilot, peering into the inky darkness.

'But, where are the lower lights?' asked the captain.

'They must have gone out, sir,' came the reply.

'Can you still make the harbour then?' enquired the now anxious captain.

'We must, or perish, sir,' said the pilot solemnly, as he swung the wheel again.

With a strong hand and a brave heart the old pilot steered the heaving vessel onward. But alas! In the darkness he missed the vital channel, the boat crashed on the rocks and many lives were lost.

When Mr. Moody first told the story of the shipwreck at Cleveland, he concluded with these words, *'Brethren, the Master will take care of the great lighthouse; let us keep the lower lights burning.'*

That story fired the imagination of one of Dr. Moody's associates, Philip Bliss. He was already a song writer and composer of some repute; and when he took the moral of this story and told it in song, it became popular immediately. Soon, *Let The Lower Lights Be Burning*, was being sung in Moody campaigns everywhere. Later it was to become a firm favourite with that other American evangelist, Billy Sunday.

We all meet with people every day, and for those people we may provide the only opportunity they will ever have to hear the gospel. Unless we tell them, they may never hear!

I'm sure that's what Philip Bliss had in mind when he penned the last verse of his hymn. In exhorting us to show others the way of salvation it speaks of lambs of a different but equally important kind, and reminds me of something from my childhood days.

I grew up on my father's small farm and one of the things I remember clearly is, the 'hurricane' lamp. Those were the days before electricity came to our part of the country, so if you had any work to do outside at night, a lamp was essential. 'Hurricanes,' were the most popular.

These had a wide metal base and a strong carrying handle; they used paraffin oil, and had a wick which was totally enclosed in a storm-proof, glass globe. Hence, the name 'Hurricane'.

From time to time, when the light would grow dim, my father would dismantle the lamps to clean them.

The glove would be washed, then polished with newspaper until it sparkled. The wick would be trimmed, removing all the charred edges, and neatly shaped to give a nice oval flame. Then the lamp would be refilled with fresh oil and lighted. It was almost a pleasure to go out on a dark, winter night with a 'hurricane' which had received this treatment.

I feel that's the type of lamp Philip Bliss was referring to when he wrote:

> *Trim your feeble lamp, my brother;*
> *Some poor sailor tempest-tossed*
> *Trying now to make the harbour,*
> *In the darkness may be lost.*

Jesus expressed the same thought in an almost identical way when He said, *'Let your light so shine before men, that they may see your good works, and glorify your Father which is in heaven.'*

> *Brightly beams our Father's mercy*
> *From His lighthouse evermore;*
> *But to us He gives the keeping*
> *Of the lights along the shore.*

> *Let the lower lights be burning!*
> *Send a gleam across the wave!*
> *Some poor fainting, struggling seaman*
> *You may rescue, you may save.*

Lord I'm Coming Home

William J. Kirkpatrick

Williiam J. Kirkpatrick was born in 1838. This man was not only a marvellous lyricist, but his musical settings for poems written by others have afforded us such favourites as *Jesus Saves* and *'Tis So Sweet To Trust In Jesus*.

Kirkpatrick was a Methodist choir director and organist, and he especially loved the Methodist camp meetings. During one such meeting, at which he directed the music, he became quite burdened because the invited soloist would sing and then immediately leave, without hearing the sermon or staying to fellowship with other Christians.

After a couple of days of this, Kirkpatrick prayed fervently that God would somehow reach this young man with the gospel of Christ. You see, he feared that the singer had never really known Christ as Saviour. As a result, God gave a beautiful song to William Kirkpatrick, which he asked the soloist to sing during an evening service of the meetings. He did so, and he was so convicted in his heart as he sang the words that he decided to stay and hear the sermon. Following the sermon, the singer knelt in the altar area and was gloriously converted.

During that notable camp meeting, near Philadelphia, Pennsylvania, the song that so moved the heart of the soloist and has been used for the Lord to do the same in thousands of hearts ever since was:

> *I've wandered far away from God,*
> *Now I'm coming home;*
> *The paths of sin too long I've trod -*
> *Lord, I'm coming home.*

Nineteen years later, at age eighty-three, Kirkpatrick was sitting up late, working on a music composition. His wife awakened and noticed that the lights were still on in his study. After calling out to him and hearing no response, she went quickly to his study and found him slumped over his last musical offering. He had gone peacefully home to his Lord.

Coming home, coming home
Nevermore to roam;
Open now Thine arms of love -
Lord, I'm coming home.

My Faith Looks Up To Thee

Ray Palmer

One day, in 1832, two men stood outside a store in Boston, Massachusetts. One was Lowell Mason, the other Ray Palmer.

Mason had just retuned from Savannah, Georgia where, for the past 16 years, he had been a choir director and bank clerk. Three years later he would be awarded the first degree of Doctor of Music conferred by an American college and would go down in history as one of the all time great hymn-tune composers.

Even now he was one of the busiest men in Boston, directing three choirs and trying to persuade the local Board of Education to put music courses on the city schools curricula. He was also currently compiling material for his new book *Spiritual Songs for Social Worship*.

Palmer, just 24 years old, had recently worked in a shoe shop; but was a graduate of Yale University and in another three years was to be ordained to the Congregational ministry.

As the two men chatted on the street Mason tackled Palmer about the possibility of him writing some verses which he, Mason, could set to music for the new book. As it happened Ray Palmer had just the very thing and he pulled a notebook from his pocket.

For 10 years Ray Palmer had burned the candle at both ends, studying for the ministry and working for his keep at the same time. Often he had wondered how long he could go on. Indeed he had been on the point of giving up more than once.

One night, just to comfort himself when he felt down and out, he wrote a poem. No one else had yet seen it but now he opened the notebook and handed it to Lowell Mason.

Mason was immediately impressed and, borrowing a sheet of paper, copied down ...

> *My faith looks up to Thee,*
> *Thou Lamb of Calvary,*
> *Saviour divine!*
> *Now hear me while I pray,*
> *Take all my guilt away,*
> *O let me from this day*
> *Be wholly thine!*

Three more equally moving and inspiring verses followed.

When he had finished Mason turned to Palmer and said, 'Mr. Palmer, you may do many good things but posterity will remember you as the author of *My Faith Looks Up To Thee.*' That same night, in 1832, Mason set Palmer's first and greatest hymn to music.

Thus a bank clerk and a shoe salesman, who stopped for a chat in Boston, gave the world a hymn and Christians everywhere have been singing it ever since.

> *May Thy rich grace impart*
> *Strength to my fainting heart,*
> *My zeal inspire;*
> *As Thou hast died for me,*
> *O may my love to Thee*
> *Pure, warm and changeless be,*
> *A living fire.*

Nearer My God To Thee

Sarah Flower Adams

I used to work as a messenger boy for a Belfast firm of industrial suppliers. One of our biggest customers was the mighty Queen's Island shipyard; so almost every week found me down there, in one department or another, delivering everything from goggles to grommets.

I used to love to walk through the busy engine works and see the building and testing of those monstrous mechanical wonders that would one day find a place in the depths of some great ocean-going vessel; driving it through the waves with speed and power.

Sometimes, on a good day, I stood and watched the actual building of a ship. It was an amazing sight for a country lad to see gigantic pieces of sheet metal being swung through the air and then gently set into place by the skill of the crane-man. To this day I can hear the deafening and monotonous rat-tat-tat of the riveting machines; and see the dazzling blue and gold flashing of the electric arc welders as, sheet by sheet, a great ship was put together.

The 'Island' is renowned for its ships; many with famous and historic names. I remember the building of the 'Canberra', and recollect how proud she looked as she lay at her moorings while being fitted out. I remember, too, the building of the first oil rig; an absolutely monstrous structure and, at that time, and eighth wonder of the world.

But I suppose the most famous, and sadly, the most tragic of all the vessels built at Belfast was the 'Titanic', which sank, on her maiden voyage, on that fateful night in April 1912.

Many stories are told about that night of terror, but surely one of the most poignant is the account of how the band, which all evening had played music to dance to, finally, just as the ship was about to slide beneath the icy waters, broke into the strains of a famous hymn.

The one they chose was *Nearer, My God, To Thee.*

The inspiration for this timeless favourite came to the author, Sarah Flower Adams, through the reading of the scriptures, in particular, the story of Jacob at Bethel. (Gen. 28:10-22). As she read the moving story, a prayer was born in her heart and she longed to be drawn near to her Lord.

Some say her minister had preached on the passage and was looking for a suitable hymn to use with it. Using her literary talents, Mrs Adams skillfully condensed the Biblical account of Jacob's dream into five stanzas. She composed the lines in November, 1840.

It was said to be the favourite hymn of President William McKinley. As he lay dying, after being shot in Buffalo, New York, he was heard to whisper, *Nearer, my God to Thee ... nearer, my God to Thee.*

Sarah Flower, as was her maiden name, inherited her love for and ability with words from her father who was a newspaper editor. She was born in England in 1805 and teamed with her sister, Eliza, in writing and publishing sacred songs. *Nearer, My God To Thee,* first appeared in 1841 in their book *Hymns and Anthems.*

It's interesting to note that the popular tune for *Nearer, My God, To Thee* Lowell Mason's *Bethany* is an arrangement of a beautiful old Irish ballad *Oft In The Stilly Night.*

Sarah Flower Adams was taken ill with, the then dreaded, consumption and passed away at the early age of forty-three.

Her hymn, however, has lived on for more than a hundred and forty years.

> *Nearer, my God, to Thee,*
> *Nearer to Thee;*
> *E'en though it be a cross*
> *That raiseth me;*
> *Still all my song shall be,*
> *Nearer, my God, to Thee*
> *Nearer to Thee.*

Now Thank We All Our God

Martin Rinkart

The text of a hymn may give us an inkling about the life and work of its writer. For instance, the chorale *'A Mighty Fortress'* reveals the cataclysmic struggle between God and satanic powers, which parallels Martin Luther's crusade against the entrenched and decadent ecclesiastics of the 16th century. Another hymn like Rinkart's *'Now Thank We All Our God'* may seem to have little connection with the period and the situation in which it was produced. Investigation into its history turns up amazing facts.

Martin Rinkart was a pastor at Eilenberg, Saxony during the Thirty Years' War (1618-1648). Because Eilenberg was a walled city, it became a severely overcrowded refuge for political and military fugitives from far and near. As a result, the entire city suffered from famine and disease. In 1637 a great pestilence swept through the area, resulting in the death of some eight thousand persons, including Rinkart's wife. At that time he was the only minister in Eilenberg because the others had either died or fled. Rinkart alone conducted the burial services for 4480 people, sometimes as many as 40 or 50 a day!

During the closing years of the war, Eilenberg was overrun or besieged three times, once by the Austrian army and twice by the Swedes. On one occasion, the Swedish general demanded that the townspeople make a payment of 30,000 thalers. Martin Rinkart served as intermediary, pleading that the impoverished city could not meet such a levy; however, his request was disregarded. Turning to his companions the pastor said, 'Come my children, we can find no mercy with man; let us take refuge with God.' On his knees he led them in a fervent prayer and in the singing of a familiar hymn, *'When In The Hour Of Utmost Need.'* The Swedish commander was so moved that he reduced the levy to 1,350 thalers.

We may well ask why all this dramatic experience and difficulty is not reflected in Rinkart's hymn. Had the good pastor seen so much stark tragedy that he had become insensitive to human needs and problems? Of course not. He simply had come to believe that God's providence is always good, no matter how much we are tempted to doubt it.

Now thank we all our God
With heart and hands and voices,
Who wondrous things hath done,
In whom His world rejoices;
Who, from our mother's arms,
Hath blessed us on our way
With countless gifts of love,
And still is ours today.

O may this bounteous God
Though all our life be near us,
With ever joyful hearts
And blessed peace to cheer us;
And keep us in His grace,
And guide us when perplexed,
And free us from all ills
In this world and the next.

All praise and thanks to God
The Father now be given,
The Son, and Him who reigns
With them in highest heaven,
The one eternal God,
Whom earth and heaven adore;
For thus it was, is now,
And shall be evermore.

O Come, All Ye Faithful

John Francis Wade

John Francis Wade was an itinerant scribe. In those days long ago, when printing was still in its infancy and a rather slow way of reproducing copies of a work, he roamed from time to time offering his services to those who could pay for them.

Wade was a craftsman of the highest order, working in several languages and able also to copy music manuscripts. Consequently, his copywriting was much in demand by choir leaders, institutions of learning, churches and wealthy families.

He worked mostly in his native England but also ventured as far afield as France and some of the Western European countries to ply his trade there.

Apparently, however, scribe Wade didn't spend all his time copying the works of others. In 1750, as part of a manuscript he prepared for a college in Lisbon, Portugal, he included an original composition from his own pen.

It was written in the Latin language and began …

Adeste, fideles,
Laeit triumphantes;
Venite, venite in Bethlehem …

In English, it's the very popular …

O come, all ye faithful, joyful and triumphant,
O come ye, O come ye to Bethlehem …

Wade also composed a fine tune for the words he had written, and when the two were blended they produced an extraordinary musical composition. It's sung with great enthusiasm in churches all over the world at Christmas.

In 1785 the carol was heard by the then Duke of Leeds. He introduced it to a group of concert singers of which he was the conductor and it increased in popularity from that time.

Eventually, it circled the globe, being translated into the language of every civilised nation on the way. In the past century for example, it has appeared in over one hundred different English translations.

However, it was not until 1852, and the translation by Canon Frederick Oakley of Shrewsbury, that it became known by its present popular title *O Come All Ye Faithful*.

It should be pointed out that some historians assert that John Francis Wade was not, in fact, the author of this carol. They say he borrowed both the words and music from others whose names we will never know.

But whether or not Wade was guilty of plagiarism, it is undeniable that this moving carol would never have come into the possession of the Christian church had he not inserted it into that ancient manuscript.

Amen! Lord we bless thee
Born for our salvation,
O Jesus! forever be Thy name adored;
Word of the Father,
Now in flesh appearing.

O come let us adore Him,
Christ the Lord!

O God Of Bethel

Philip Doddridge

This famous hymn takes us into midland England, to the boot and shoe making town of Northampton where in 1730 Philip Doddridge began his ministry of twenty-one years.

Most likely the hymn arose out of a sermon based on Genesis 28: 20-22 for Doddridge had an original way with his congregations. At the end of a sermon he would recite a hymn connected with it, and get his congregation to repeat it line by line. Few of them, of course, could read and write so a hymn-book would not have been very helpful. One member of his church, however, did copy down the Doddridge hymns, over five hundred of them. This hymn has been rewritten first by John Logan and then by the Scottish Paraphrases of 1781.

Doddridge himself was only forty-nine when he died in 1751 but his Northampton ministry set a standard of piety and thoroughness for the ministry of the Free Churches in England.

He was a friend of Isaac Watts and this hymn is a close companion to *Our God Our Help In Ages Past*. Both men were not only pioneers in hymn-writing, but they realised that worshippers would naturally make hymns their prayers and meditations at the same time. In fact they were authors of 'prayer-books' as much as hymn-books, although neither of them set out consciously to make a hymn-book.

> *O God of Bethel! by Whose hand*
> *Thy people still are fed;*
> *Who through this weary pilgrimage*
> *Hast all our fathers led;*

Our vows, our prayers, we now present
Before Thy throne of grace;
God of our fathers, be the God
Of their succeeding race.

Through each perplexing path of life
Our wandering footsteps guide;
Give us each day our daily bread,
And raiment fit provide.

O spread Thy covering wings around,
Till all our wanderings cease!
And at our Father's loved above
Our souls arrive in peace.

Such blessings from Thy gracious hand
Our humble prayers implore;
And Thou shalt be our chosen God
And portion evermore.

O Little Town Of Bethlehem

Phillips Brooks

The Reverend Phillips Brooks spent Christmas 1865 in Bethlehem, the town where the baby Jesus was born. The sights and sounds of the ancient city flooded into his keen mind leaving indelible impressions. Three years later these impressions would be enshrined in a hymn he would write specially for the children of his Sunday School.

Phillips Brooks was a big man, physically, mentally and spiritually. He is said to have been one of the biggest preachers of his day, standing six foot six in height with a weight to match. Clint Bonner tells us that *'he sang 200 hymns from memory and blasted out sermons at a rate of 250 words per minute.'*

The story of the hymn he wrote goes back to a December day in 1868 when the massive preacher paced the study of the Episcopal Church in Philadelphia, where he was the minister.

It was just a few days before Christmas; and Brooks was working on a sermon appropriate to the season. Out in the church the organist and Sunday School superintendent, Lewis Redner, practised carols and special music for the coming Christmas services.

As the preacher walked up and down, his thoughts took him back to Bethlehem and the shepherds watching over their sheep, just as they did when Jesus was born.

Eventually, he laid aside his sermon preparation and took up his pen. The words: *O little town of Bethlehem, how still we see thee lie* flowed quickly and in a short time he had completed the four verses.

He then asked Redner to write a tune. The organist made no claim to be a composer but agreed to have a go. The days passed, until it was almost Christmas, but Redner still didn't have any ideas for the music. Then something quite amazing happened!

On the eve of Christmas day, just about midnight, he was awakened, 'as *thought by an angel strain. The music seemed to come down from heaven,'* he later recorded. Quickly he jotted down the melody, then, just as quickly as he was awakened, he went back to sleep. Next morning he finished the harmonies for the tune and later that same day taught the new carol to the children of the Sunday School.

It must have been a great thrill for those children to sing *O Little Town Of Bethlehem,* the first time it was ever heard on that Christmas day in 1868.

Phillips Brooks continued his ministry for another 25 years, eventually becoming Bishop of Massachusetts. He remained a bachelor; but never lost his love for, and way with, children. It seems they loved him too, for, when he died, in Boston in 1893, one little 5-year-old girl said, with tears in her eyes, *How happy the angels will be.*

The angel's gain was the children's loss. But at least Bishop Brooks left something really precious to be remembered by.

O little town of Bethlehem,
How still we see thee lie!
Above thy deep and dreamless sleep
The silent stars go by:
Yet in thy dark streets shineth
The everlasting Light;
The hopes and fears of all the years
Are met in thee tonight.

O Love That Wilt Not Let Me Go

George Matheson

We often wonder why it is that God allows His saints to suffer so much hardship. Yet, it's true that He does. The latter part of Hebrews chapter eleven is proof positive, if such proof is needed, that this is so.

However, God has a purpose in everything. He doesn't do things by whim or by chance. Everything is reasoned and planned, and for the very best of motives. When he does ask His child to endure hardship, it is never out of malice or spite, but that the believer may learn to trust Him more.

Yet, it's wonderful how so many of these trials become triumphs; and how seemingly impossible situations turn into milestones of blessing.

Surely, one such is the experience which led George Matheson to write those lovely words, *O Love That Wilt Not Let Me Go*.

George Matheson was born in Glasgow, Scotland, on 27th March, 1842. Before he was very old it was discovered that he suffered from a disease which would eventually cause him to become completely blind. Despite this, he pressed on with his studies, and, in due course entered university, graduating with honours, when he was 19.

It was while at university that he suffered the stunning blow which later prompted the writing of his beautiful hymn.

He had met and fallen in love with a young woman, also a student at the university, and, in due course, they planned to be married. But then George had to tell her the awful news that one day he would be blind! Would she still marry him?

To his astonishment and grief her blunt answer came, striking to his heart with the force of a dagger: *I do not want to be the wife of a blind man.'* And with that they parted.

Years later the memory of that rebuff came flooding back on the eve of his sister's wedding; and in less than five minutes he penned those immortal words.

Matheson recorded that they were *'the fruits of suffering, written when I was alone and suffering a mental anguish over something that no one else knew.'*

This story will surely strike a sympathetic chord in the heart of every reader. Who among us would care to suffer the deep personal hurt which was George Matheson's; yet who among us has not been blessed with the words which were born out of that desperate experience?

That George Matheson triumphed over his great disappointment is evident. After leaving university he spent another four years in the study of theology, preparing himself for the ministry.

His first pastorate was at Innellan on the Clyde, where he stayed for 18 years. It was while there that he received a summons to preach before Her Majesty Queen Victoria. The Queen was so impressed by his preaching and prayers that she presented him with a small sculpture of herself. She had the thoughtfulness not to present a blind man with a photograph.

His ministry continued, long, faithful and fruitful, until August 28th 1906, when, on a much needed holiday, he was called home to be with his Saviour. His body was laid to rest in the family vault at Glasgow.

Some would say that much of the success of *O Love That Wilt Not Let Me Go*, results from the tune 'Saint Margaret.' It was composed by Dr. Albert L. Peace; who was organist at Glasgow Cathedral and it came to him while sitting on the sandy shores of the Arran Island.

> *O love, that wilt not let me go,*
> *I rest my weary soul in Thee;*
> *I give Thee back the life I owe,*
> *That in Thine ocean depths,*
> *Its flow may richer, fuller be.*

Once For All

Philip P. Bliss

Elsewhere in this book I make the point that Wales is 'The Land of Song.' It's equally true to say that Scotland is the land of Psalm singing.

I've spent many a happy day in Scotland. I love its ancient traditions, its fascinating history, its beautiful lochs and rivers, and its heather clad mountains and hills.

Most of all I love its wonderful people, so warm-hearted, hospitable and generous. All those stories you hear about Scots' meanness are just not true!

I love their Psalm singing too. Whether it be around the fireside as they conduct family worship, or in the church on the Sabbath, there's a reverence about the way they sing the psalms. They sing them with such simplicity (there's no instrumental accompaniment) and yet they sing them with such sincerity and devotion.

To this day, in Scotland, many of the churches sing only the psalms in public worship. But back in the days when D.L. Moody and his friend Ira D. Sankey came to Scotland for an evangelistic campaign, psalm singing was in predominance throughout the churches.

You can imagine, then, with what fear and trepidation Sankey got up to sing his gospel solos. Once, a woman had stormed out of the service protesting that 'The devil was in his kist (chest) o' whistles.' Such was her opinion of Sankey's little pedal organ.

Mr. Sankey's concern was heightened one night when he observed that the great Scottish preacher and hymn-writer Horatius Bonar was in the audience. This is how Sankey recounted the story in his book. *My life and the story of the gospel hymns:*

> Of all men in Scotland he was the one concerning whose decision I was most solicitous. He was, indeed, my ideal

hymn writer, the prince among hymnists of his day and generation. And yet he would not sing one of his beautiful hymns in his own congregation ... because he ministered to a church that believed in the use of the Psalms only.

With fear and trembling I announced as a solo the song, 'Free from the Law, oh, happy condition.' Feeling that the singing might prove only an entertainment and not a spiritual blessing, I requested the whole congregation to join me in a word of prayer, asking God to bless the truth about to be sung. In the prayer my anxiety was relieved. Believing and rejoicing in the glorious truth contained in the song, I sang it through to the end.

At the close of Mr. Moody's address, Dr. Bonar turned to me with a smile on his venerable face, and reaching out his hand he said: 'Well, Mr. Sankey, you sang the gospel tonight.' And thus the way was opened for the mission of sacred song in Scotland.

This hymn, written by Philip Bliss, who's mentioned elsewhere in this book, contains the whole message of the gospel. It's a wonderful statement of faith and includes the whole story of sin and death, of grace and salvation purchased *once for all* by the death of the Saviour.

What better appeal could have been made to those Scots Presbyterians that this thoroughly orthodox statement of the gospel?

Free from the law, O happy condition!
Jesus hath bled, and there is remission;
Cursed by the law and bruised by the fall,
Grace hath redeemed us once for all.

Once for all - O sinner receive it!
Once for all - O brother believe it!
Cling to the cross, the burden will fall;
Christ hath redeemed us once for all.

Onward! Christian Soldiers

Sabine Baring-Gould

I t was a sunny Sunday morning on August 10, 1941. The British battleship *Prince of Wales* was at anchor in the spacious Placentia Bay, Newfoundland, and on her wide quarter-deck a happy crowd of British and American sailors were gathered for church parade. Facing the great camouflage guns were sitting two famous men - Franklin Roosevelt and Winston Churchill - singing heartily with the sailors,

> Onward! Christian soldiers,
> Marching as to war,
> With the cross of Jesus
> Going on before.

Together the two men had chosen the hymns for this church parade at which the American and British sailors stood shoulder to shoulder, a symbol of what was to come later in the same year.

Churchill's choices were *Our God Our help In Ages Past*, and *Onward Christian Soldiers*. Roosevelt pleaded for *Eternal Father Strong To Save*, too, and so the three great hymns rose through the still morning air at this historic meeting where the Atlantic Charter was signed.

After he returned home across the dangerous ocean waves Churchill broadcast to the British people about the hymn singing:

'We sang *Onward Christian Soldiers* and indeed, I felt that this was no vain presumption but that we had the right to feel that we were serving a cause for the sake of which a trumpet has sounded from on high. When I looked upon that densely packed congregation of fighting men of the same language, of the same faith, of the same fundamental laws, of the same ideals ... it swept across me that here was the only hope, but also the sure hope, of saving the world from measureless degradation.'

So the hymn which Baring-Gould wrote in 1865 for his Sunday School children to march to in their procession through the village street of Horbury Brig was lifted on this occasion to a marching song for all the free peoples.

The hymn's third verse,

We are not divided,
All one body we,
One in hope and doctrine,
One in charity

was certainly written with an eye on the Horbury children as they marched in unity and unison. No doubt it was that vision too which inspired Winston Churchill as he looked over the quarter-deck of the *Prince of Wales* on that sunlit morning in 1941 and saw the young sailors of the old and new worlds standing and singing together.

O Perfect Love

Dorothy F. B. Gurney

Thousands of people at thousands of weddings must have sung this popular and moving hymn, without knowing the simple story behind its composition.

O Perfect Love, was written in 1883, by Dorothy Frances Bloomfield Gurney; and all in the space of about fifteen minutes. According to Mrs Gurney, relating the story afterwards, it happened like this:

It was Sunday evening and we were enjoying a time of hymn singing. A song that was particularly enjoyed by us all was O Strength And Stay. As we finished someone remarked, 'What a pity the words of this beautiful song are not suitable for a wedding!'

My sister turned to me and challenged, 'What's the use of a sister who composed poetry if she cannot write new words to a favourite tune? I would like to use this tune at my wedding.'

I picked up a hymnbook and said, 'If no one will disturb me, I'll go into the library and see what I can do.' Within fifteen minutes I was back with the group and reading the words I had jotted down. The writing of them was no effort after the initial idea came to me., I feel God helped me to write this song.

Some two or three years after its original composition, O Perfect Love, found its way into the well known hymnal, Hymns, Ancient and Modern. Possibly because of this, it soon became popular, especially in London, where it was used at many fashionable weddings, including those of royalty.

In 1889, Sir Joseph Barnaby composed a new tune with the appropriate name Sandringham and the hymn was sung to this tune when Princess Louise of Wales, daughter of King George V, was married to the Duke of Fife.

Since then the hymn has been translated into many languages and has attained worldwide fame. Mrs Gurney's sister had her ambition realised too, for it was also sung at her wedding.

Spiritual insight into the meaning of hymns isn't always easy. However, in his book *The Gospel In Hymns* Albert Bailey points out that in this hymn, 'the Lord Jesus Christ is given two titles that are of special significance in marriage - *'perfect love'* and *'perfect life'*. He concludes that these titles speak of two great ideals which are important in every marriage; *motive* and *performance*. If these ideals are honoured and obeyed they will yield joy and peace in any marriage.

Perhaps it's also worth noting that Mrs Gurney certainly brought out the truth that human love cannot begin to compare with God's love; which 'transcends all human thought'.

Mrs Gurney died in 1932 and the London Times printed a tribute to her in the words with which I began this story. 'Thousands of people at thousands of weddings must have sung, or heard sung, *O Perfect Love*, without ever knowing that Mrs Gurney was the writer.'

O perfect Love, all human thoughts transcending,
Lowly we kneel in prayer before Thy throne,
That theirs may be the love which knows no ending
Whom Thou for evermore dost join in one.

O That Will Be Glory

C. H. Gabriel

It is often difficult to predict whether or not a new hymn will 'catch on' with the public. Actually, only a small number of those that are published ever reach a second edition. Of the 6500 hymns written by Charles Wesley during the 18th century, probably no more than 200 are sung anywhere today. Even so, this is a remarkable record of poetic longevity that is not equated by any other hymnwriter.

When *O That Will Be Glory* first appeared in 1900, a musical expert predicted, 'It will never go. It has too many quarter notes.' In other words, 'the rhythm is too monotonous.' But in a few years, it was the most popular hymn Homer Rodeheaver led in the Billy Sunday campaigns. It was affectionately called the *Glory Song* and was inspired, not by an experience, but by a personality!

The author, C.H. Gabriel, was perhaps the best known and most prolific gospel song writer of the early twentieth century. One of his good friends was Ed Card, superintendent of the Sunshine Rescue Mission of St. Louis, Missouri. Ed was a radiant believer who always seemed to be 'bubbling over' with Christian joy. During a sermon or a prayer he would often explode with 'Glory!' just as some people say 'Amen!' or 'Hallelujah!' His beaming smile earned him the nickname 'old glory face.' It was his custom to close his fervent prayers with a reference to heaven, usually ending with the phrase 'and that will be glory for me!'

> *When all my labours and trails are o'er*
> *And I am safe on that beautiful shore,*
> *Just to be near the dear Lord I adore*
> *Will through the ages be glory for me.*

O that will be glory for me,
Glory for me, glory for me,
When by His grace I shall look on His face,
That will be glory, be glory for me!

When by the gift of His infinite grace
I am accorded in heaven a place,
Just to be there, and to look on His face,
Will through the ages be glory for me.

Friends will be there I have loved long ago;
Joy, like a river, around me will flow;
Yet just a smile from my Saviour, I know,
Will through the ages be glory for me.

O Worship The King

Robert Grant

Everybody has heard of the great Austrian composer Franz Joseph Haydn, who lived from 1732-1809.

Haydn was one of the great composers of all time and is credited with, among other things, the invention of the modern string quartette.

Not many people, however, have heard of his equally musical brother, Johann Michael Haydn.

Both were the sons of a wheelwright who was also a great lover of music. He played the harp without knowing a note of music and when the boys were small he taught them to sing.

When Franz Joseph was only seven years old the chapel-master heard his weak but pleasant voice and put him in the choir at St. Stephens in Vienna.

There, until he was 18, he sang soprano, but then, his voice changed and his singing career ended. His younger brother, however, took his place and learned the same musical and composing skills.

Between the two of them, the brothers Haydn gave to the world some of the finest music ever to fall upon the ears of man.

Amongst other things, Johann Michael wrote some 360 pieces of music for the church.

He was past middle age and an accomplished composer when a child was born to a Member of Parliament in Scotland.

When he grew up, Robert Grant followed his father into Parliament and into the East India Company, of which his father was chairman. He too became a director of the company and was eventually appointed governor of Bombay and given a knighthood.

Mr. Grant Sr. had encouraged the sending of missionaries to India. His son, Robert did more. He supported the missionaries and wrote hymns for them to sing. He wrote little but he wrote well.

Sir Robert Grant died in 1839 but a year later his twelve hymn-poems were published through the good offices of his brother Charles. They were given the not too original title *Sacred Poems*.

Set to various tunes they found their place in a number of hymnals but none of them ever took the world by storm. None, that is, except this one.

Based on the words of Psalm 104 the hymn exhorts us:

O worship the King all glorious above,
And gratefully sing his wonderful love;
Our shield and defender, the Ancient of Days,
Pavilioned in splendour, and girded with praise.

As you can see, Sir Robert had a way with words, and the rest of the hymn continues in the same vein.

Thy bountiful care what tongue can recite?
It breathes in the air, it shines in the light,
It streams from the hills, it descends to the plain,
And sweetly distils in the dew and the rain.

This hymn always reminds me of the years I spent at grammar school in Belfast. It seems as though we sang it almost every week in that most wonderful of public school traditions, morning assembly.

I'm sure our rendering of it was by no means melodious but it certainly left a lasting impression upon me.

Some say that the majestic words written by the governor of Bombay would never have become popular but for the beautiful tune written by the son of an Austrian carriage wheel maker.

For my part, I agree that the words and music combine beautifully, but have no doubt that the words by themselves would stand up very well. They are, after all, a paraphrase of the Word of God.

Praise My Soul The King Of Heaven

Henry Francis Lyte

Based on the 103rd Psalm, Henry Lyte's stately hymn of praise has probably begun more solemn ceremonies than any hymn in the English language. Lyte himself is of course more immediately connected with his hymn *Abide With Me* but the story of his hymn-writing goes back to the time when he was a curate at Marazion in Cornwall where he had come after his college days in Dublin. There, when he was twenty-five, he had a deep religious experience caused by the illness and death of a brother clergyman.

This experience turned Lyte from being a conventional and formal clergyman, with a gift for versifying, into a poet with a religious message. He says that the death of his friend 'who died happy in the thought that there was *One* who would atone for his delinquencies' made him 'study my Bible and preach in another manner than I had previously done'.

This free paraphrase of Psalm 103 was published in his book *Spirit of the Psalms* in 1834 when he was in his ministry at Brixham, the Devon fishing port. The Brixham fishermen are famous for their gallantry and daring in the stormy waters of the Atlantic fishing grounds, and Lyte's hymn has something of the tenderness of strong men in dangerous places.

> *Father-like He tends and spares us;*
> *Well our feeble frame He knows:*
> *In His hands He gently bears us,*
> *Rescues us from all our foes:*

The hymn was chosen by Queen Elizabeth for her wedding to the Duke of Edinburgh on November 20, 1947 - also the day of the centenary of Lyte's death.

Lyte captures the measure of the Psalm in unforgettable verses. It has time, eternity, God and man all locked in its embrace, and its last verse has the soaring quality of high religion. In one grand sweet the writer brings the whole created universe into the act of praise.

> Angels, help us to adore Him,
> Ye behold Him face to face;
> Sun and moon, bow down before Him.
> Dwellers all in time and space:
> Praise Him! praise Him!
> Praise with us the God of grace!

Rock Of Ages

Augustus M. Toplady

The Rev. Augustus Montague Toplady, is one name which must be included in any list of the great hymn writers.

One day Toplady was travelling through the pleasant English country-side when a sudden, fierce storm sent him scurrying for shelter. He found it nearby, in the cleft of a great rock.

There are several places throughout Britain and Ireland where local people will point positively to the exact location of Toplady's place of refuge. However, since it's such a matter of uncertainty and dispute I'll refrain from favouring any one in particular.

The important thing is that the great man found the shelter he needed; and the wonderful thing for us is that, while there, and inspired by the situation and surroundings, he penned those immortal lines: *Rock of ages cleft for me, let me hid myself in thee.*

The Rev. Toplady was also the editor of a little religious periodical entitled, *The Gospel Magazine*, and sometime later he used the lines he had written beneath the shelter of the rock in an article he had prepared for that paper.

In this he sought to establish the utter sinfulness of man and the absolute necessity of receiving Christ's pardon. It was a totally scriptural essay and to prove his point he compared the sins of the average individual to the national debt of England.

Toplady had calculated that a fifty year old man in his lifetime would be guilty of; one billion, five hundred and seventy-six million, eight hundred thousand sins. He quite rightly argued that it was humanly impossible for anyone to pay off such a staggering debt of iniquity. Therefore, sinners must needs avail themselves of the mercy and pardon of the Lord Jesus, who died upon the Cross to 'redeem us from the curse of the law.'

He concluded the article with - 'A living and dying prayer for the holiest believer in the world' - which contained the recently written hymn *Rock Of Ages.*

Just two years after those blessed words were first published, Augustus Toplady, at only 38 years of age, passed from this scene of time, into eternity; and to the everlasting shelter of *The Rock of ages.*

Rock of Ages, cleft for me - Psalm 62: 5-8
Let me hide myself in Thee - Exodus 33: 22
Let the water and the blood - 1 John 5: 6
From Thy riven side which flowed - John 19: 34
Be of sin the double cure - 2 Kings 2: 9-10
Cleanse me from its guilt and power - Isaiah 1: 19

Not the labour of my hands - John 5: 30 (first clause)
Can fulfil the law's demands - Exodus 33: 22
Could my zeal no respite know - Psalm 69: 6 (first clause)
Could my tears forever flow - Psalm 6: 6
All for sin could not atone - Heb. 10: 5-6
Thou must save and Thou alone - Hebrews 10: 8-10

Nothing in my hand I bring - Isaiah 4: 1
Simply to Thy Cross I cling - Galatians 6: 14
Naked come to Thee for dress - Rom. 13: 14 (first clause)
Helpless look to Thee for grace - Philippians 4: 13
Foul, I to the fountain fly - Psalm 2: 7
Wash me Saviour, or I doe - John 13: 8 (second clause)

While I draw this fleeting breath - Psalm 103: 15-16
When my eyelids close in death - Ecclesiastes 12: 3-7
When I soar to worlds unknown - John 14: 2-3
See Thee on Thy judgment throne - Matthew 25: 31
Rock of Ages cleft for me - 1 Corinthians 10: 4 (third clause)
Let me hide myself in Thee - Psalm 16: 1-8

Silent Night

Josef Mohr

The annual presentation of the Christmas story was to be held in St. Nicholas Church in the tiny village of Oberndorf, near Salzburg, in the Austrian Alps. The actors discovered that the church organ was broken and so presented the show in a private home. The assistant pastor, Josef Mohr attended and began to reflect on the real meaning of the Christmas season.

Mohr strode to a hillside overlooking the village as it lay shrouded in a still, clear night. Words began to form in his mind - the verse of *Silent Night, Holy Night*. He later presented the verses to the church organist, Franz Gruber, a schoolmaster and songwriter. It is reported that Gruber composed the musical setting the same day he received Mohr's poem.

On Christmas Eve that year, Gruber and Pastor Mohr sang the song to the little congregation gathered in the church. The organ was still in ill repair, forcing Gruber to accompany them on his guitar.

This carol was a favourite from the beginning. Soon, Austrian concert singers, the Strasser Sisters, began singing it throughout Europe. From there it has orbited the earth again and again. It was translated into English from the Austrian language in 1863 by Jane Campbell and made its first appearance in America in 1871 in Charles Hutchin's *Sunday School Hymnal*.

Silent Night, Holy Night is one of those carols that 'wears like steel.' It is as fresh and beautiful today as the first time it was played and sung that Christmas Eve in a little Austrian town more than 170 years ago.

Silent night, holy night,
All is calm, all is bright,
Round yon Virgin Mother and Child
Holy Infant, so tender and mild,
Sleep in heavenly peace,
Sleep in heavenly peace.

Softly And Tenderly Jesus Is Calling

Will Thompson

Will Thompson came out of the state of Ohio where his birthplace was East Liverpool. His musical gifts took him eastwards to Boston and its Conservatory of Music, and two of his songs won more than local fame. But Thompson's heart was in melody's linked to Christian words, and with *Softly And Tenderly* he made a memorable contribution to the revival songs of America at a time when D. L. Moody was leading his evangelical campaigns.

> *Softly and tenderly Jesus is calling*
> *Calling for you and for me,*
> *See, on the portals He's waiting and watching,*
> *Watching for you and for me.*

Moody loved this hymn-melody so much that he told Thompson as he lay dying that he would rather have written it than have done anything else.

> *Come home, come home,*
> *Ye who are weary*
> *Come home.*
> *Earnestly, tenderly, Jesus is calling,*
> *Calling, O sinner come home.*

Thompson himself died in 1911 at the age of sixty-two.

Stand Up, Stand Up For Jesus

George Duffield

Preaching against slavery wasn't a popular thing to do in many parts of the USA during the early 1850's. An awful civil war, brought about by division over that very issue, was looming.

However, Dr. Dudley Tyng, the twenty-nine year old rector of the Church of the Epiphany in Philadelphia, passionately believed that slavery was 'immoral and unchristian,' so he denounced it.

He also believed that all men are sinners by nature and need to repent and be converted if they are ever to enter heaven.

Dudley Tyng was no ordinary church pastor and this bold, straightforward denunciation of sin disturbed his cultured and wealthy parishioners so much that by the end of his second year in the church many were demanding his removal.

Tyng resigned from the rich and fashionable assembly and formed his own 'Church of the Covenant' which met for worship in a little meeting hall. With his wife and boys, he went to live on the family farm outside Philadelphia.

At the same time he also began giving lectures at the Philadelphia YMCA. Interest grew and thousands were converted to the Saviour. At one particular meeting held in Jayne's hall in March 1858, 5,000 men were present.

During his address Dr. Tyng said, 'I must tell my master's errand and I would rather this right arm were amputated at the trunk than I should come short of my duty in delivering God's message.'

Those words were strangely prophetic, for just the next week, while watching a horse-powered cornsheller at work on the the farm, he was caught in the wheels of the machinery and his right arm was badly mangled.

A few days later it was necessary to amputate at the shoulder.

Tyng was dying - and he realised it. As the loved ones gathered around his bed he took his father by the hand and addressed the old man, who was also a faithful preacher. in these words.

Stand up for Jesus father, stand up for Jesus
and tell my brethren of the ministry,
wherever you meet them, to stand up for Jesus.
And thus he died.

The dying exhortation impressed another of Tyng's ministerial colleagues, the Rev. George Duffield. He took up the theme in a sermon preached the following Sunday from Eph. 6: 14: 'Stand therefore, having your loins girt about with truth.' At the close of the sermon he read the words of this hymn he has composed just after Dr. Tyng's funeral.

Stand up, stand up for Jesus
Ye soldiers of the cross
Lift high His royal banner
It must not suffer loss
From victory unto victory
His army He shall lead
'Till every foe is vanquished
And Christ is Lord indeed.

Sweet Hour Of Prayer

William Walford

I n Lord Tennyson's poem 'Morte D'Arthur'
there's a line which reads:
'More things are wrought by prayer than this world dreams of.'
    Certainly, nothing is accomplished in the Lord's work without prayer. It
is the very life of it.
    How much we need to pray, and yet, must we not confess - how little we
do pray? I suppose then, every encouragement of prayer is valuable, even
essential. This hymn is just that.
    William Walford of Coleshill, England was a wood-carver by trade and
the owner of a small trinket shop. He was also a devout Christian and often
the guest preacher in the churches around the area where he lived.
    One day, in 1842, the Reverend Thomas Salmon, a congregational
minister, made his customary call at the shop of a friend. On this occasion,
instead of showing the minister his beautiful collection of hand carved
ornaments, Walford asked Mr. Salmon to write down the words of a poem
he had just completed.
    The first verse went like this:-

Sweet hour of prayer, sweet hour of prayer
That calls me from a world of care
And bids me at my Father's throne
Make all my wants and wishes known
In seasons of distress and grief
My soul has often found relief
And oft' escaped the tempter's snare
By thy return, sweet hour of prayer

Three years later the Reverend Salmon was in New York city and, while there, took the old wood-carver's poem along to the editor of the *New York Observer*, As a result, *Sweet Hour Of Prayer* appeared in the issue for September 1845.

Nothing happened for another fourteen years. Then the famous composer, William Bradbury, set the poem to music and turned it into one of the most famous hymns of all time.

Lifted on the wings of Bradbury's beautiful melody the words soon sped around the globe and in a short time were being sung by millions.

I mentioned earlier that William Walford had asked the minister to write down the words of his poem for him. The simple reason for this was that Walford himself was blind - he couldn't see to write.

He wasn't blind spiritually though. The eyes of his soul could see perfectly clearly. It took a rate insight to write such a meaningful and blessed sacred song as this.

Sweet hour of prayer, sweet hour of prayer
Thy wings shall my petition bear
To Him whose truth and faithfulness
Engage the waiting soul to bless;
And since He bids me seek His face,
Believe His word, and trust His grace,
I'll cast on Him my every care,
And wait for thee, sweet hour of prayer!

Tell Me The Old, Old Story

Katherine A. Hankey

Williiam Ewart Gladstone, one time Prime Minister of England, was lecturing on the subject of 'Science, Industry and Art.'

During his speech he said, 'I do not mention any of these things as the great remedy for relieving the sorrow of human life and combating the evils which defile the world. If I am asked what is the remedy for such things, I must point to something which, in a well known hymn, is called *The Old, Old Story*, told of in an old, old book, and taught with an old, old teaching, which is the greatest gift ever given to mankind.' A tremendous tribute, from a great statesman, to the lady who penned the words of this hymn.

Katherine Arabella Hankey was the daughter of a prosperous banker. She belonged to a group who sought to apply the ethics of Christ to personal, social, political and national affairs, and, like her father, showed great interest in people who were less fortunate than herself. she devoted much time to Bible teaching, especially among the factory girls of that day, and her efforts were rewarded in that many of her students became leaders in Christian work.

In 1866 Katherine, or Kate as she was better known, suffered a serious illness which required a lengthy convalescence. As she lay thinking of the story of redemption, she longed for someone to come in and tell her the old, old story. As a result she wrote a two-part, 50 verse poem on the life and work of our Lord. Part One was called *The Story Wanted* and contained the words of this hymn *Tell Me The Old, Old Story*. Part Two entitled *The Story Told* included a companion song, *I Love To Tell The Story*.

Written especially for children, *The Old, Old Story* has been translated into more languages than almost any other children's hymn. The blessing of it has gone far beyond those for whom it was intended, for people of all ages and all in all circumstances have known its touch. It seems clear then, that Katherine Hankey's intention was more than fulfilled.

Speaking of the purpose behind the hymn she said 'God's remedy for sin is something I want to understand, and I want to hear it often, lest I forget it. As weak as I am, I cannot think too well or too fast. I need to have the story explained to me as a little child.'

Tell Me The Old, Old Story has a beautiful, gently flowing, and easily remembered tune. It was composed by Dr. William Howard Doane, whose interests included cotton manufacturing, woodworking, and the invention of much of the machinery used in those businesses.

Of the melody he composed to accompany these words he said, 'I was attending the international Convention of the Young Men's Christian Association. Among those present was Major-General Russell, then in command of the English forces during the Irish home rule excitement. When the General rose to speak, he did not discuss the Irish situation, as we had expected. Simply and very softly he said, 'I merely want to read a very beautiful poem which should be the dominant theme undergirding everything we do here.' Then he read the words of Miss Hankey's hymn. At the end of the poem, General Russell was too emotional to speak.'

Dr. Doane continued 'So impressed was I with the words that I requested a copy. Later, when travelling between the Glen Falls House and Crawford House in the White Mountains, I composed a tune for the words and added a simple little chorus. That evening, in the hotel parlours, we sang, *Tell me the old, old story*, to my new tune.

> *Tell me the old, old story*
> *Of unseen things above,*
> *Of Jesus and His glory,*
> *Of Jesus and His love,*
> *Tell me the story simply,*
> *As to a little child;*
> *For I am weak and weary,*
> *And helpless and defiled.*
>
> *Tell me the old, old story,*
> *Tell me the old, old story,*
> *Tell me the old, old story,*
> *Of Jesus and His love.*

Tell Mother I'll Be There

Charles M. Fillmore

Tell mother I'll be there, in answer to her prayer,
This message, blessed Saviour, to her bear!
Tell mother I'll be there, heaven's joys with her to share,
Yes, tell my darling mother I'll be there.

These lines form the chorus of a hymn that's a great favourite with many people.

I can never hear it without thinking of a dear soul I knew many years ago. She was a pitiful creature; continually in the grips of alcohol and slowly being destroyed by its power. On more than one occasion I picked her up by the roadside, sometimes bedraggled and wet, ol times unable to stand on her feet, always drunk, and took her home.

Eventually I got a call one day to tell me that she had been pulled out of the river. Would I conduct the funeral ceremony?

What a sad occasion it was for her aged father with her brothers and sisters stood around the open grave to bid their last farewells.

The reason I am reminded of all this is that every time I rescued Ruth in her drunken state she would be singing the words of this chorus, *Saviour, Tell My Mother I'll Be There.*

Tell Mother I'll Be There, was written by the hymn-writer Charles M. Fillmore and is said to have been inspired by an incident in the life of President William McKinley.

McKinley was a devout Christian. He taught a Bible class and was superintendent of a Methodist Sunday School. He was also devoted to his mother!

Not many people knew that every day of his mother's life William McKinley either saw, wrote to, or telegraphed her.

When she became seriously ill, in the winter of 1897, he had her home in Canton, Ohio connected to the White House by special telephone. He also kept a train standing by, under full steam, 24 hours a day.

Eventually, the call came, Mother McKinley asked for her famous son, and attendants sent the message, 'Mr President,we think you had better come.' From the president's office this answer was flashed back - *'Tell mother I'll be there.'*

On Sunday afternoon, December 12th 1897, Nancy McKinley breathed her last.

Less than four years later, on September 6th 1901 when attending the Pan-American exposition in Buffalo NY, McKinkey was cut down by a bullet from the gun of anarchist Leon Czolgosz.

Eight days later, on September 14th, President William McKinley passed into the presence of his Lord and was reunited with the mother to whom he had been so devoted.

His last words - 'God's will be done'; his last request - the sounds of a hymn his mother had taught him, *Nearer My God To Thee.*

The King Of Love My Shepherd Is

Henry Williams Baker

If down the years the great Shepherd Psalm has been turned and twisted to suit the generations and their singing capacities, no one did it more happily than Sir Henry Williams Baker in this hymn. He devoted his life (1821-77) to hymns, and stayed for twenty-six years as vicar in the little village of Monkland amongst the apple orchards of England's Herefordshire in order that he might write hymns and edit hymn-books.

For years he worked on the first comprehensive hymn-book that was offered to the Church of England, which has won such a place of affection for itself, *Hymns, Ancient and Modern,* and was himself a prolific contributor to it.

Baker's rendering of Psalm 23 is his monument. It has as easy swing about it.

> The King of love my Shepherd is,
> Whose goodness faileth never;
> I nothing lack if I am His,
> And He is mine, for ever.
>
> Where streams of living water flow
> My ransomed soul He leadeth,
> And, where the verdant pastures grow,
> With food celestial feedeth.

Verse three is particularly expressive of the Good Shepherd.

Perverse and foolish oft I strayed,
But yet in love He sought me,
And on His shoulder gently laid,
And home, rejoicing, brought me.

These were the last words that Baker spoke as he lay dying - as tender a verse as any written in the hymn-books.

The Old Rugged Cross

George Bennard

The famous gospel singer George Beverley Shea, narrates a lovely introduction to this hymn on one of his records. He says:

> 'I was just a small boy in Winchester, Ontario, and one day two fine singers, from the USA, came to our home and asked my mother to play for them, while they sang a song they said was new, The old rugged cross. I stood transfixed, near the piano, and watched their faces as they described, in this tender song, the suffering of the Lord. At a later time, I came to know the wonder of God's forgiveness.'

I, too, can remember distinctly the first time I heard this great hymn.

As a young lad I went with my mother on what we called a 'bus run'. That's a special outing, usually to the seaside and travelling, in those days before cars were so numerous, by special, privately-hired bus. A great treat indeed!

To occupy the time on these jolly jaunts there would always be a bit of a sing-song. The popular tunes of the day, the beautiful old Irish ballads and everyones' favourites would be enthusiastically aired.

To this day I carry a clear mental picture of an old cream and green bus, chugging its smokey way along a twisting country road, its cargo of carefree passengers packed like sardines and singing like thrushes.

But even more clear is the memory of the hymn, for, always on those occasions the singing would end and the day be brought to a close, as if to pour a sanctifying oil over the whole proceedings, with a hushed and reverent rendering of a favourite hymn. The one which I can remember above all others is 'The Old Rugged Cross.'

The author and composer Rev. George Bennard, testifies that this hymn was not born in haste. He prayerfully read everything the Bible has to say about the cross of Christ and thus became convinced that the cross was not just a religious symbol. It was, rather, the very heart of the gospel of the Lord Jesus; the only gospel by which poor sinners are saved.

George Bennard believed that redemption for man only comes through Christ's sacrifice on the accursed tree.

Gripped by the vision of redemption, the theme of *The Old Rugged Cross* came to him. The words however, were not written until after a two-week waiting period which he described as a 'test of faith.'

He had already composed that unique melody, and now the words were wedded to it; a beautiful and perfect union.

On a hill far away stood an old rugged cross,
The emblem of suffering and shame;
And I love that old cross where the dearest and best
For a world of lost sinners was slain.

So I'll cherish the old rugged cross
Till my trophies at last I lay down:
I will cling to the old rugged cross
And exchange it someday for a crown.

The Solid Rock

Edward Mote

It's many years now since I first heard a preacher recite the rather unusual couplet:

On Christ the solid rock I stand;
All other rocks - are shamrocks!

He was quoting, of course, from a parody on the chorus of the hymn *On Christ The Solid Rock I Stand.*

What a fine hymn that is, Bishop Bickersteth, himself an outstanding hymnist, called it 'a grand hymn of faith'. There's no doubt that his assessment is right.

The Solid Rock, to give the hymn its proper title, was written in 1834 and first appeared, anonymously, in leaflets and newspapers. Very quickly, considerable debate arose as to the identity of the author, and so the man responsible, Mr. Edward Mote, decided to acknowledge his workmanship.

Explaining how the idea for the hymn came - on his way to work - Mote said, 'I began to meditate on the gracious experience of the Christian, soon the chorus, and then the words of the first verse, came to mind.'

The following Sunday, coming out of morning worship, he was invited to a friend's home to encourage his wife who was critically ill. He went to the home in the early evening, and after spending some time comforting the dying woman was asked to join in family worship.

It was the custom in the house to sing a hymn, read the scripture, and then pray. As the man of the house searched in vain for a hymn book, Edward Mote said, 'I have some verses in my pocket. If you like we can sing them,' and they did.

The new words struck a responsive chord in the heart of the sick woman and, as a consequence, her husband requested a copy for her.

'Back at home,' continues the author, 'I sat by the fireside, musing on the sick lady's reaction to the words I had written; and soon the entire hymn was clear in my mind.'

This new, enlarged version was committed to paper and a copy made for the dying friend. Later, he decided that, since the hymn had been such a blessing and comfort to this woman in her last hours, maybe it would be of help to others as well.

Edward Mote was born in London on January 21st 1797. His background appeared to be far from Christian. As a boy he had no interest in the things of God. In fact, so ignorant was he of spiritual matters that he didn't even know there was a God.

His parents were of no help to him either. They kept a public house and sent their son to a school where the Bible was neither taught nor permitted. On Sundays, instead of attending church, he and his friends spent their time playing in the streets. Such was his irreligious, unsheltered upbringing.

However, for some reason which is not known, Edward began attending church when he became apprenticed to a cabinet maker. Around about this time he went to hear the famous preacher, Rev. John Hyatt at Tottenham Court Road Chapel. Mote records that the sermon made him 'think on his way', and two years later he came into the experience of salvation.

Eventually, he felt called to preach the gospel which he now so passionately believed; and was instrumental in the building of at least one church. It is evident that he exercised a faithful ministry there for, when he died, the congregation erected a plaque which included in the inscription these words:

For 26 years the beloved pastor of this church, preaching Christ and Him crucified, as all the sinner can need, and all the saint can desire.

Assurance and security were Edward Mote's constant companions throughout his long life. Even when his health began to fail and he was approaching death he felt a renewed confidence in the merit of the blood of Christ.

Just before he died, in 1874, he said, 'I think I am nearing Port. But the truths I have preached I am living upon, and they will do to die upon, Ah! the precious blood! The precious blood which takes away all my sins; it is this which makes peace with God.'

And thus Edward Mote, preacher and hymn-writer said farewell to this earth ...

Dressed in His righteousness alone,
Faultless to stand before the throne!
On Christ, the solid rock I stand
All other ground is sinking sand.

The first verse and chorus of the hymn is ...

My hope is built on nothing less
Than Jesus' blood and righteousness
I dare not trust the sweetest frame,
But wholly lean on Jesus' Name.

On Christ the solid Rock, I stand;
All other ground is siniing sand.

The Sweet By And By

Sandford F. Bennett

Just like all the rest of us, composer Joseph Webster had his off days. So when he walked into the office of his friend Dr. Sandford Bennett, the doctor instinctively knew that the musician was down in the dumps.

'What's the trouble now,' Bennett asked Webster, who appeared rather melancholy.

'Oh, nothing,' came the dejected reply. 'Everything will be alright by and by.'

Dr. Bennett turned back to his desk where he wrote prescriptions as a profession and verse as a hobby. 'By and by', he mused. *The sweet by and by.* He paused, looked over at Webster who by this time was warming himself at the stove and then reached for his writing paper and pen.

The man at the stove, Joseph Philbrick Webster was an out and out musician. In the east, where he was born in 1819, he had been an active member of the Handel and Hayden society and a prolific composer of popular songs. In his early thirties he made the great move west, first to Indiana and then in 1857 to Elkhorn, Wisconsin, where he eventually settled.

When the verse writing physician, Sandford Fillmore Bennett moved to the same town in 1861, it was natural that the two should strike up a partnership.

After six years Bennett knew Webster like a song-book and he soon learned that the best remedy for his partner's bouts of gloom was a batch of verses to be set to music.

But on that particular day in 1867, the clever doctor had no such remedy in stock. However, Webster's casual remark had given him a theme and quickly he had gone to work.

While the physician wrote hastily at his desk two other townsfolk joined the musician at the stove. In a few minutes Bennett handed Webster three verses and a chorus; and in less time than it had taken the doctor to write the words the composer set it to music.

He gave the melody a few rounds on his violin and the four men sang the new hymn for the first time.

There's a land that is fairer than day,
And by faith we can see it afar,
For the Father waits over the way
To prepare us a dwelling-place there

In the sweet by and by,
We shall meet on that beautiful shore.
In the sweet by and by,
We shall meet on that beautiful shore.

To our bountiful Father above
We will offer the tribute of praise,
For the glorious gift of His love,
And the blessings that hallow our days.

There Is A Fountain Filled With Blood

William Cowper

Mention has already been made, in this book, of William Cowper, English poet and hymn writer who lived from 1731 until 1800.

It was Cowper, working in collaboration with the great John Newton, who complied and produced *Olney Hymns* a publication to which he personally contributed at least sixty-four original hymns.

There Is A Fountain Filled With Blood, is his most famous; but before we can tell the story of the hymn it is necessary to set the scene by looking briefly at the life of the man himself.

William Cowper was born in Great Berkhampstead in Hertfordshire in November 1731. His mother died when he was only six years old and this tragedy left a life-long scar of grief. When he was ten he was sent to boarding school and there his suffering was added to by the cruelty of the older boys.

However, he survived and at eighteen began to study law. Although he passed all the bar examinations he never achieved much success in his profession. In nine years of law practice, so-called, Cowper never once felt worthy to serve people nor could he manage to attract business for himself.

Next, a clerkship in the House of Lords was arranged for him, but still he felt unfit for the task and was in such misery that he made several attempts to take his own life. The failure of these suicide efforts, compounded by two unhappy love affairs, increased his feelings of self contempt; so that as he walked the streets he felt that all eyes were fixed upon him in scorn.

Because of his suicidal tendencies Cowper was confined, for a brief period, in St. Albans Asylum and, remarkably, it was during this time that his famous hymn was written.

A visiting relative sought to ease the sick man's depression by telling him of Jesus' power to save. Cowper burst into tears saying, 'It is the first time that

I have seen a ray of hope.' When the friend had gone the poet opened his Bible at random and, in the providence of God, his eyes fell on those words in Romans Ch. 3 v 25: 'Whom God hath set forth to be a propitiation through faith in his blood.'

This scriptural account of Christ's redeeming work touched Cowper's heart, causing him to later testify thus:

There shone upon me the full beams of the sufficiency of the atonement that Christ has made; my pardon in His blood; the fulness and completeness of my justification and, in a moment, I believed and received the gospel.'

So thrilled was he by his new-found hope that he described it in verse, basing it on the words of Zechariah Ch. 13 v 1: 'In that day there shall be a fountain opened up for sin and uncleanness.'

There is a fountain filled with blood,
Drawn from Immanuel's veins;
And sinners plunged beneath that flood
Loose all their guilty stain.

It was William Cowper's great hope that other troubled souls would be helped by his hymns.

Surely it must be said that he has succeeded far beyond his wildest expectations. How many countless thousands have been helped, blessed and encouraged by the singing of *There Is A Fountain Filled With Blood*.

Personally, I never like to conduct a gospel meeting without singing at least one hymn about the blood of Christ, and this is one of my favourites.

The great 'Prince of preachers', Charles Haddon Spurgeon was so taken with the words of this hymn that instructions were given for some of the lines to be inscribed on his tomb. To this day visitors to the Spurgeon grave at Norwood cemetery, South London, can read:

E're since by faith I saw the stream
Thy flowing wounds supply
Redeeming love has been my theme,
And shall be till I die.

What better way to sum up the whole theme of the hymn than by quoting

Dear dying Lamb! Thy precious blood
Shall never lose its power,
Till all the ransomed church of God
Be saved to sin no more.

There Is A Green Hill Far Away

Cecil Frances Alexander

The Cathedral Church of St. Columb in Londonderry, N. Ireland, occupies the highest ground within the old walled city. The tall spire atop the building makes a fine outline against the blue sky on a clear day; nothing else interrupts the view.

St. Columb's has stood on its commanding site for more than 350 years and is fair steeped in history.

Within its Chapter House are a host of relics dating back to the time of the famous siege of 1688-1689. Then it was that upwards of 30,000 Protestants from the surrounding area packed into the ancient city; to seek shelter behind its stout walls from the approaching armies of King James II.

The walls of the Chapter House are lined with cupboards and cabinets, each crammed with memorabilia of the siege. The locks and keys of the sturdy wooden gates; pistols and muskets used in defence of liberty; even a piece from the tree, down which a traitor is said to have escaped. All are there to delight and amaze!

But all these took little of my attention when I visited the place some time ago. My interest, then, was taken by a picture which has pride of place on one wall. It's the picture of a woman, saintly of face, modest of dress, and by all reports, gracious of spirit.

Cecil Frances Alexander, for that's the lady in the picture, is remembered with affection in the city which was once her home.

In the baptistry of the cathedral a beautiful memorial window, fashioned in stained-glass, pays eloquent tribute to her life and witness.

Mrs Alexander lived and worked for the sake of children, and so it is fitting that she should be especially remembered there.

The scene of the window, portrayed in gorgeous colours, depicts the Saviour's love and care for little ones; and the simple inscription at the bottom reads:

In grateful memory of Cecil Frances Alexander, wife of William, Bishop Alexander. She died in this city on 12th October 1895.

Besides the window a large plaque, which has been skillfully worked to have the appearance of a tapestry, displays one of Mrs Alexander's finest pieces of poetry *A Prayer for this Cathedral church*. It includes this telling verse:

> Be here 'O Christ of our Salvation,
> As once in Israel's temple fair;
> Cleanse Thou from sin our poor bolation,
> And make this house a house of prayer.

It is for her poetry that Mrs Alexander will be best remembered, especially the songs written for children.

As early as 1848 she published her famous little volume: *Hymns for little children*, which she dedicated thus:

'To my little Godsons, I inscribe these lines hoping that the language of the verse, which children love, may help to impress on their minds what they are, what I have promised for them, and what they must seek to be.'

She went to great pains to write some 41 hymns for the spiritual edification of her little friends and it's interesting to note the plan she adopted.

As the basis of her songbook she took the catechism and wrote verses on each section of it, thus hoping to impress its truths upon young hearts. In the book there are hymns on the Trinity, Baptism, The Creed, the Ten Commandments, and The Lord's Prayer.

Among the well known favourites are *Do Not Sinful Action; All Things Bright And Beautiful; Once In Royal David's City* and *There Is A Green Hill Far Away*.

The inspiration for this last hymn is said to have come from the neighbourhood where she lived although, it must be added, there are conflicting accounts of how the hymn was suggested to her.

The Alexanders lived in the Bishop's Palace, almost beside the cathedral. The house had a commanding view out over the city walls to the green hills beyond. No wonder then that she was inspired to write:

There is a green hill far away,
Without a city wall,
Where the dear Lord was crucified,
Who died to save us all.

By 1872 *'Hymns for little children'* had sold 414,000 copies, clear evidence of its blessing to multitudes.

Mrs. Alexander died on October 12th, 1895 some 16 years before her husband.

He eventually became Archbishop of Armagh and Primate of all Ireland and when that appointment took place moved to live in the city of Armagh, ecclesiastical seat of Ireland.

But the Primate was a Derry man at heart and longed to come home again someday. It is said that he always wished to be buried in his native city with his feet towards the river Foyle. His wish was granted.

The Alexanders lie buried on the slope of that 'green hill' which inspired the writing of the lovely hymn. A plain white marble cross marks the spot.

Beneath the name Cecil Frances Alexander is written in brackets:

(C.F.A., Hymn writer)

On that great day, when we all stand before the judgment throne of heaven, surely all will rise up and call her, 'blessed'.

Thine Be The Glory

Edmund Budry

The writer Edmund Budry was pastor for thirty-five years at Vevey on Lake Geneva, and wrote over sixty hymns many of which appeared in the hymn-book *Chants Evangeliques*.

Thine Be The Glory was written in French in 1884.

> *A toi la gloire O Ressuscite*
> *A toi la victoire pour l'eternite.*
> *Brillant de lumiere, l'ange est descendu,*
> *Il roule la pierre du tombeau vaincu.*

which Richard Birch Hoyle translates

> *Thine be the glory, Risen conqu'ring Son,*
> *Endless is the vict'ry Thou o'er death hast won.*
> *Angels in bring raiment rolled the stone away,*
> *Kept the folded grave-clothes, where Thy body lay.*

The translator of this hymn, R.B. Hoyle (1875-1939), was an English Baptist minister with remarkable linguistic gifts. His free translations always manage to capture the spirit of the original, as in verse two.

> *Voi-le paraitre: C'est lui, c'est Jesus,*
> *Ton Sauver, ton Maitre! Oh! ne doute plus;*
> *Sois dans l'allegresse - People du Seigneur,*
> *Et redis sans cesse - Que Christ est vainqueur!*

> *Lo Jesus meets thee - Risen from the tomb;*
> *Lovingly He greets thee - Scatters fear and gloom;*
> *Let His church with gladness - Hymns of triumph sing,*
> *For her Lord now liveth; Death has lost its sting.*

To God Be The Glory

Fanny Crosby

I f a hymn can die, can it live again? The life story of 'To God Be The Glory' proves that the answer is 'yes!' Originally composed in America sometime before 1875, it was almost immediately forgotten in its native land. In 1954, however, *To God Be The Glory* was rediscovered and claimed as a new favourite.

Cliff Barrows, Billy Graham's song leader explains: 'It was suggested that we include *To God Be The Glory* in a song-book we were compiling for the London crusade of 1954. Because of its strong text of praise and its attractive melody, I agreed. We introduced the hymn during the early days of those meetings in Harringay Arena. As a result, Billy Graham asked that we repeat it often because he was impressed with the enthusiastic participation of the audience. In the closing weeks of the crusade it became our theme hymn, repeated almost every night. The words well expressed our praise to God, who was doing wondrous things in Britain.'

Returning to America, we brought the hymn with us and used it first in Nashville, Tennessee crusade of August, 1954. It was quickly adopted by many church groups and has recently been included in several new hymnals.

Why *To God Be The Glory* was so late in achieving recognition in its homeland may always remain a mystery. It is not mentioned in the writings of either Fanny Crosby, author of the words, or W. H. Doane, composer of the music. Evidently the songleader Ira D. Sankey took it to Great Britain when he went there with evangelist D. L. Moody in 1873. Sankey included it in his *Sacred Songs and Solos* a hymnbook first published in England in 1874 and still in use today.

For some unknown reason, the song did not appear in the important *Gospel Hymns* series of books which Sankey published in America after his returning from Britain in 1875. Through the years, *To God Be The Glory* has been included in several American hymnals. But until 1954 it failed to find its rightful place in the singing of our congregations.

To God be the glory, great things He hath done,
So loved He the world that He gave us His Son.
Who yielded His life an atonement for sin,
And opened the Lifegate that all may go in.

O perfect redemption, the purchase of blood,
To every believer the promise of God;
The vilest offender who truly believes,
That moment from Jesus a pardon receives.

Great things He hath taught us, great things He hath done,
And great our rejoicing thro' Jesus the Son;
But purer, and higher, and greater will be
Our wonder, our transport, when Jesus we see.

Trust And Obey

John H. Sammis

The music for this song was composed by D. B. Towner, the first director of music at Moody Bible Institute in Chicago. The inspiration for the hymn's writing came in 1886 during an occasion when Towner was leading singing for D.L. Moody in Brockton, Massachusetts. In a testimony service which took place, he heard a young man say, 'I am not quite sure - but I am gong to trust, and I am going to obey.'

Towner jotted down the words and sent them to his friend J.H. Sammis, a Presbyterian minister, who developed the idea into a full hymn. the refrain came first - it is a capsule version of the entire song.

Trust and obey,
For there's no other way
To be happy in Jesus,
But to trust and obey.

The song emphasises the two aspects of being a Christian - faith and good words. And it places them in proper order! We come to Christ without any plea 'but that He had shed His blood' for us.

But *after* we trust in Christ, our faith must be translated into action. Because God loves us and we love Him, we seek to obey Him, and do His will in every realm of our lives. As James asks, 'What use is it for a man to say he has faith when he does nothing to show it?'

When we walk with the Lord
In the light of His Word,
What a glory He sheds on our way,
While we do His good will
He abides with us still,
And with all who will trust and obey.

Trusting Jesus

Edgar Stites

*T*rusting *Jesus* is a hymn that is completely American in background. Edgar Stites, author of the words, was a direct descendant of John Howland, one of the Mayflower's passengers. Active in the Civil War, he was later a riverboat pilot and then a missionary to the frontier churches in South Dakota.

The hymn poem first appeared in a newspaper, and was handed to the American evangelist D.L. Moody. In turn, Moody gave it to his soloist and songleader, Ira D. Sankey, asking him to set it to music. In his book, *Sankey's Story of the Gospel Hymns*, the singer says, 'I assented, on condition that he should vouch for the doctrine taught in the verses, and he said he would.'

This hymn was the favourite of Dr. W.B. Riley, and it expresses well the motivating purpose of his life. During the more than forty years that Dr. Riley was the beloved pastor of the First Baptist Church in Minneapolis, Minnesota, he was a pillar of strength in the evangelical movement.

The frequent theme of Dr. Riley's preaching was the grace of God. He both taught and lived a practical Christianity that is proclaimed in this motto and title: *Trusting Jesus, That is All.*

Simply trusting every day,
Trusting through a stormy way;
Even when my faith is small,
Trusting Jesus, that is all.

Brightly doth His Spirit shine
Into this poor heart of mine;
While He leads I cannot fall;
Trusting Jesus, that is all.

We Love The Place, O God

William Bullock

In the middle of the nineteenth century as a young naval officer William Bullock was a member of a survey expedition along the coasts of Newfoundland. While he was map-making, charting and sounding the depths he was also observing the life of the people. Their poor condition, an isolation from the rest of the world, and lack of religious worship and instruction so depressed him that he left the navy and went back to the bleak coasts as a missionary.

On Trinity Bay he built his first little church, and for it he wrote the hymn which as been more often sung at church dedications than any other. Few men get a chance of building a church, and fewer still write the one hymn which fits the occasion.

> We love the place, O God,
> Wherein Thine honour dwells;
> The joy of Thine abode
> All earthly joy excels.
>
> It is the house of prayer,
> Wherein Thy servants meet;
> And Thou, O Lord, art there,
> Thy chosen flock to greet.

What A Friend We Have In Jesus

Joseph Scriven

Only the Lord and the man in question really know what burdens of sorrow and affliction were heaped upon the writer of this great hymn. One thing we do know, however, is that this beautiful and blessed hymn would never have been penned if the author had not known such trouble.

The man was Joseph Scriven and he was born near Banbridge, in the heart of the rolling hills of County Down, Northern Ireland.

After graduating from Dublin's famous 'Trinity College' he seemed set for a brilliant career and a happy life for he was also engaged to be married.

But then tragedy struck! His fiancee was accidentally drowned on the very eve of their wedding and Joseph Scriven was plunged into his first great experience of sorrow. In the providence of God it was this tragedy which brought him to a personal knowledge of Jesus Christ.

In 1845 Scriven sailed for Canada to start life anew and, hopefully, to leave all his sorrows behind. But it was not to be, for ill-health dogged him and he was forced to return to Ireland after only two months.

Two years later he again set sail for Canada to take up a teaching post. In this he was successful and later graduated to the position of private tutor to the children of a military captain.

Life, at last, seemed worth living and prospects were continually improving!

Again he met and fell in love; this time with a charming young woman of twenty-three. Soon they were engaged to be married.

However, bitter disappointment was once more to be his unhappy lot, for this young lady was suddenly stricken with a serious illness and died before their marriage vows could be solemnised.

Cheated, for the second time, out of the prospects of a happy marriage by the cruel hand of death Scriven, quite naturally, became the victim of severe depression and declining health. But despite all this he never gave up his personal faith in the Saviour.

By this time he had settled in Port Hope, Ontario, and was manager of a small dairy there. He became known as the local 'Good Samaritan', helping the poor and under-privileged, sharing his food with the needy and often giving them clothing.

However, all these good deeds may well have been forgotten if Joseph Scriven had not written twenty-four lines of poetry to comfort his mother who was suffering from a serious illness.

Through his trials and afflictions Scriven had come to know the Lord in a very personal way, not only as Saviour but also as a friend.

Thus, from the heart he could write:

What a friend we have in Jesus,
All our sins and griefs to bear,
What a privilege to carry,
Everything to God in prayer.

As I say, Scriven wrote these words to comfort his ageing mother at a time of illness. He had not seen her since he had said 'goodbye' over ten years before and wasn't able to make the long journey back home to be with her.

So he wrote *What A Friend We Have In Jesus*, and sent it with the prayer that it would remind her of 'the never failing friend,' Jesus Christ. I'm sure it did.

Joseph Scriven never intended his poem to be published but a friend who visited him during his last illness discovered the lines and asked 'Who wrote these beautiful words?' Scriven's modest reply was 'The Lord and I did it between us.'

Soon it was published in *The Port Hope Guide,* a local newspaper. Remarkably, a copy of that newspaper was used to wrap a parcel destined for an address in New York City. when the recipient unwrapped his parcel he caught sight of Scriven's poem and arranged to have it published.

Eventually, it was seen by German-American composer, Charles Converse and very soon his simple, plaintive melody gave wings of song to Joseph Scriven's telling words.

Thus an Irish-Canadian and a German-American were used of God to bring blessing and encouragement to millions.

When I Survey The Wondrous Cross

Isaac Watts

When teenager Isaac Watts complained to his father about the monotonous way Christians in England sang the Old Testament Psalms, his father, a leading deacon, snapped back 'All right young man, you give us something better.'

To Isaac Watts, the singing of God's praise was the form of worship nearest to Heaven and he went on to argue: 'It's performance among us is the worst on earth.' Young Isaac accepted his father's challenge and eventually wrote a total of more than 600 hymns, earning him the title 'The father of English hymnody.'

Even as a child Isaac had shown a passion for poetry, rhyming and such mundane things as everyday conversation. His serious-minded father, after several warnings, decided to spank the rhyming nonsense out of his son. But the tearful Isaac helplessly replied,

'Oh father do some pity take,
and I will no more verses make.'

However, choirs, congregations and individual Christians rejoice to this day that the young lad did not keep his impromptu promise. If he had, none of us would have the thrill of singing such all-time favourites as *Oh God Our Help In Ages Past, Am I A Soldier Of The Cross* or *Joy To The World.*

As a child, Isaac Watts was sickly and unattractive, yet, even by today's standards he was clever beyond his years. He began the study of Latin at the age of four, and added Greek when he was nine, French at eleven and Hebrew at thirteen.

At fifteen the young poet turned his talents to the service of the church and the great career in hymn-writing began.

In his hymns Isaac watts takes the Word of God, of which he must have been a diligent student, and distils it so that all is wisdom, beauty and comfort are set before us with plainness and power. No wonder, then, that C.H. Spurgeon's grandfather, himself a great preacher, and in the line of the Puritans, would have nothing else but the hymns of Isaac Watts sung in his services.

Isaac Watt's greatest composition must surely be *When I Survey The Wondrous Cross*.

It has been called 'The very best hymn in the English language' and in it Watts, using only 16 lines, paints a soul-stirring picture of the Saviour's death on the cross coupled with the whole-hearted response of the believer to such amazing love.

As Tedd Smith says 'It seems to me that Isaac Watts wrote this text as if he were standing at the foot of Christ's cross.'

How blessed to reflect on the finished work of Christ Jesus, as summed up in those lines:

> *See, from His head, His hands, His feet,*
> *Sorrow and love flow mingled down;*
> *Did e'er such love and sorrow meet,*
> *Or thorns compose so rich a crown?*

And how enriching to be able to voice our reconsecration to the Lord's service in the words:

> *Were the whole realm of nature mine,*
> *That were an offering far too small;*
> *Love so amazing, so divine,*
> *Demands my soul, my life, my all.*

When The Roll Is Called Up Yonder

James M. Black

As a young man James Black was a Sunday School teacher in a church in Canada. One day me met a girl fourteen years of age, poorly clothed and the child of a drunkard. It was evident that she did not enjoy the nicer things of life that many teenagers enjoyed. Young Black was moved to invite her to attend Sunday school and to join the young people's group. He thought this would be a great blessing and help to her, and might even win her to Christ.

One Sunday, when each member answered the roll call by repeating a Scripture text, the girl failed to respond. This situation brought the thought to Black's mind that it would be a very sad thing if our names are called from the Lamb's Book of Life in heaven and we should be absent. The thought, although not theologically sound, brought this prayer to the lips of Black: 'Oh, God, when my name is called up yonder, may I be there to respond!'

He then longed for something suitable to sing, but found nothing in the books at hand. he closed the meeting that night and, while on his way home, was still wishing that there might be a song that could be sung on such an occasion. All of a sudden the thought came: 'Why don't you write it?' He tried to dismiss the idea, thinking that he could never write such a song.

When Black reached his house, his wife saw that he was deeply troubled and questioned him about his problem, but he did not reply. He only thought of the song that he would like to write. All of a sudden, like a dayspring from on high, the first stanza came in full. He later said that in fifteen minutes he had composed the other two verses. He then went to the piano and played the music just as you will find it in the hymnbooks today - note for note. It has never been changed.

When the trumpet of the Lord shall sound and time shall be no more,
When the morning breaks eternal, bright and fair;
When the saved of earth shall gather over on the other shore,
And the roll is called up yonder, I'll be there.

When the roll is called up yonder,
When the roll is called up yonder,
When the roll is called up yonder,
When the roll is called up yonder,
I'll be there.

James M. Black was born in Scotland on February 22, 1882. He was kidnapped at the age of eight and brought to Canada, where he was found by an aged minister and taken to the minister's home. It was not until he was seventeen years of age that he returned to his native Scotland and was reunited with his father and began to be active in Christian service.

Sometime later he returned to America. While on board the ship, on the way over, he heard the news that his home had been burned. Out of this experience came his other beautiful song *Where Jesus Is 'Tis Heaven There*. He died in a car accident in Colorado in1948 but will always be remembered for his songs, most especially for *When The Roll Is Called Up Yonder*.

Who Would True Valour See

John Bunyan

John Bunyan! What a wealth of history, romance, suffering, conflict and adventure is summed up at the mention of that famous name. Yet over it all can be written one qualifying word - achievement.

To write a total of sixty books in a lifetime of as many years, and with little formal education, is an achievement by itself.

To influence so many through the power of those writings is a further great achievement.

To help secure religious freedom in English law despite having absolutely no legal training is another mighty achievement.

But to prepare to spend twelve years in prison rather than compromise one's religious convictions, and yet come out joyful and unembittered surely that's the greatest achievement of all.

All this, and much more, is true of that amazing man they called *The Tinker of Bedford*.

John Bunyan was born on November 30th 1628, to Thomas and Margaret Bunyan of Elstow, near Bedford, England.

The times then were not good, by any means.

The Pilgrim Father's had departed, for freedom's sake, to America eight years earlier. In the 'New World', they found the liberty for which they longed.

At home in Britain, however, things were different. In Ireland religious unrest was the order of the day. Up in Scotland the Presbyterians were battling for their freedom. And in England itself, the Puritans were suffering tough times under King Charles.

Into such a turbulent world as this the young Bunyan was ushered. So perilous were those times that even as his father looked into the cradle where his new-born son lay he mused 'I wonder what kind of world this little one will live to see?'

Young Bunyan learned to read and write at his mother's knee and then, when he was 10 years old, was sent to the Grammar School at Bedford, to study under Master Vierney.

Vierney was a King's man, a Royalist, out and out and sought to bully all his scholars into the same position. But his efforts had no effect on John who, from his parental grandfather, had espoused the cause of the Roundheads and Cromwell.

He served in Cromwell's army for a time during the first phase of the English Civil War (1642-47), but never saw much action. However, one incident was dramatic in bringing him to realise the brevity of life and the importance of salvation.

He was invited to the birthday party of the young woman whom he eventually married. It was his night to be on guard duty at the camp and so, in order to have the time off, he asked a friend, Frederick Sheppard, to swap duties with him.

That night Royalist soldiers made a raid some distance from the barracks. A number of Royalists were killed - and one Parliamentary guard, Frederick Sheppard.

When John heard the news he was broken hearted, realising that the young colleague had died in his place.

Captain Miles, the garrison commander, lost no time in pressing home to John's softened heart the more important truth that another had also died in his place - Jesus Christ, the Saviour.

Eventually, through a long series of circumstances and the good witness of his wife, John Bunyan came to know Jesus in a real, personal, living way.

However, life as as Christian was no bed of roses for him. John Bunyan really suffered for his faith and convictions.

After the return of King Charles life for dissenters, like Bunyan, was intolerable. The authorities refused to grant such men, who weren't part of the established church, licenses to preach. Many of them, including Bunyan, were arrested, convicted and imprisoned.

Bunyan himself spent twelve years in all in the old prison at Bedford.

But they turned out to be twelve of the most fruitful years of his life for, in prison, he took up the pen and by that pen influenced more people than he ever could have done had he been left at liberty to preach.

Ever since his boyhood Bunyan had been a dreamer. In fact he's often referred to as *The Immortal Dreamer*. There in Bedford jail he was to dream his greatest dream of all.

The Pilgrims Progress, tells the story of *Christian's* journey from the City of Destruction to the Celestial City and pictures the journey of the believer through this life to heaven at last.

In the story, one of the characters, *Christiana* and her four sons are near their goal when they meet a wounded man on the street. His name is *Mr. Valiant-for-Truth*. They wash his wounds, give him food and drink and learn his story as they travel onwards together.

Mr. Valiant-for-Truth had set out on the journey to the Celestial City because of the example of *Christian* and now he relates his experiences of obstacles and battles along the way. And then, since pilgrims love to sing, they all launch into song together.

> *Who would true valour see,*
> *Let him come hither;*
> *One here will constant be,*
> *Come wind, come weather,*
> *There's no discouragement*
> *Shall make him once relent*
> *His first avowed intent*
> *To be a pilgrim.*

It's a tremendous hymn calculated to inspire the most doubtful spirit; the most disconsolate soul and to rekindle the fire of zeal and enthusiasm for the pilgrim journey. Clearly, it's a hymn born out of Bunyan's own trials and struggles ... *to be a pilgrim.*

God's ways are not our ways and nowhere is this more clearly demonstrated than in the life of John Bunyan.

Work For The Night Is Coming

Annie Walker Coghill

Work, for the night is coming,
Work through the morning hours;
Work while the dew is sparkling,
Work 'mid springing flowers;
Work when the day grows brighter,
Work in the glowing sun;
Work, for the night is coming
When man's work is done.

Annie Louise Walker, who was later to marry Harry Coghill, was only eighteen when she wrote the words of this famous gospel hymn. It is based on John 9: 4, 'The night cometh when no man can work.' She was born in England, but later lived in Canada, and it was while in Canada in 1854 that the hymn was written, probably under the sense of the pioneering necessity of work, and more work, which helped to lay the foundations of Canada in the late nineteenth century.

Work till the last beam fadeth,
Fadeth to shine no more,
Work, while the night is dark'ning
When man's work is o'er

It is said that she disliked Lowell Mason's setting of her song, but his vigorous music has helped to give *Work, For The Night Is Coming* a firm tread which goes well with the words.